SHAKESPEARE
AND PLATONIC
BEAUTY

SHAKESPEARE
AND PLATONIC
BEAUTY

John Vyvyan

1961
CHATTO & WINDUS
LONDON

Published by
Chatto & Windus Ltd
London
*
Clarke, Irwin & Co. Ltd
Toronto

To my Sons
ANTHONY & DESMOND

CONTENTS

I find the whole in elusive fragments: let one
    be caught
And profoundly known—that way, like a
    skeleton key, the part
May unlock the intricate whole. What else is
    the work of art?

C. DAY LEWIS

I son colui che ne' prim anni tuoi
Gli occhi tuoi infermi volsi alla beltate
Che dalla terra al ciel vivo conduce.

It was I, Love, who in your youth, turned
your feeble sight to Beauty; and that will
lead you, living from earth to heaven.

MICHELANGELO

Chapter I

THESEUS AND HIPPOLYTA

THE figures of Theseus and Hippolyta, firmly enthroned, save *A Midsummer Night's Dream* from dissolving into moonlight. They are never led astray by the fairies, and they give the play substantiality. This is more than a stage impression, the stiffening is also intellectual. When Theseus hears the story of the night's confusions, his comment is, "More strange than true—". But Hippolyta insists that it "—grows to something of great constancy". The play itself does that. But what is the thing of constancy? The brief answer, I think, is beauty. That may sound deceptively simple; for behind it lies a great part of the Neo-Platonist philosophy of the Renaissance.

Why did Shakespeare chose Theseus and Hippolyta to frame his dream-story? This is the kind of question we ought to ask whenever he brings in mythological figures; because they are always more than ornament, they are part of his parable as well. The Theseus-and-Hippolyta theme—as it is presented to us here—is the turning of a war into a wedding, a sword into a ring: out of chaos has come a birth of beauty. It is to this that the regal couple in the background owe their stability. For the symbolic purpose of this play they have attained the thing of constancy towards which the wavering characters are shown to grow.

This miracle—the bringing of order out of confusion

7

—is performed by love. In Theseus and Hippolyta we see it as achieved; while in the bewildered lovers it is gradually taking place. The principle holds throughout Shakespeare's comedies. And again we touch a subject where philosophy and drama meet.

Considered philosophically, love and beauty were invented by Plato. And whenever the European mind has theorized about them since—until the Freudians set a cat among the pigeons—some echo of the *Symposium* or the *Phaedrus* is nearly always to be caught. Even during the centuries when these dialogues were lost, their influence was felt through intermediaries; and when the Platonic revival came in the Renaissance, they pervaded the thinking of the age. The result was not Platonism, but a radical re-interpretation of it, fused with much else, into a brilliant new amalgam of ideas.

In the first speech of the *Symposium*, love is said to be the unbegotten power that arose from Chaos in the beginning to create an ordered world; and in the *Phaedrus* it is a longing that will not rest until man has discovered and become united with immortal Beauty. Both these conceptions—love as creator, and revealer —are important in the Renaissance, but altered by their passage through many lively minds. From the point of view of our present enquiry, the most notable minds linking Plato with Shakespeare are Plotinus, Ficino and Spenser. These we shall consider individually. But what must never be forgotten, in spite of all the newness of the Renaissance, is the background power of medieval thought; because it is due to this that "Platonism" in the fifteenth and sixteenth centuries is so confusingly different from the classical philosophy of the same name.

Socrates speaks of the ascent of love, and Dante of its pilgrimage. Shakespeare uses both metaphors, but he prefers the more dramatic idea of love's testing. Pilgrimage and testing are contributions from medieval religion and drama, and both are valuable to a playwright. But incomparably the most important and striking bequest of the Middle Ages is the heroine: no pretty lady could have insinuated herself into "Platonism"—still less have been enthroned there—but for the prestige of centuries of courtly love.

A Midsummer Night's Dream, besides everything else that it has to offer, presents a parable. The parable is based on Platonist ideas, but it is erected in a romantic shape that Socrates would have found trivial. Romance was not trivial to Shakespeare. Long before his time, a poetic and mystical tradition had so raised its status that it had become a serviceable vehicle for philosophy: and in studying Shakespeare's romantic parables, we might perhaps adapt the exclamation of Troilus— "This is and is not Plato!"

As soon as the scene has been established by Theseus and Hippolyta, we have a love-test. The union of a pair of lovers, Lysander and Hermia, is opposed by parental and legal authority. If Hermia refuses to give Lysander up, she will either be put to death, or forced to take the veil:

> For aye to be in shady cloister mewed,
> To live a barren sister all your life.   I. i

What ought the lovers to do? Nowadays, we have been

so conditioned to accept the rightness of free choice in love that we may not notice that there is an ethical problem. But this is quite a recent outlook. In Shakespeare's time, even sweethearts would have granted that parents and the law had a certain claim upon their duty, and this consideration is a part of their dilemma. Shakespeare often presents this situation. It is more than a dramatic *cliché*: it is the problem of Juliet and of Desdemona. And the answer he gives to it is always the same—the highest duty is to love.

Is this mere romanticism? I think it can be shown to be a great deal more. But before attempting to interpret the parable—if there is one—some simpler explanations must be given due weight.

From the point of view of the theatre, Shakespeare took this basic pattern—young love in conflict with old authority—from Terence. In *The Lady of Andros*, which all Elizabethan schoolboys knew, two pairs of lovers are thwarted by their well-meaning elders; and at the close of a cleverly plotted and amusing story, harmony is made to reign. Terence, with a feeling that is remarkably modern, is always on the side of love, and the sympathies of the audience are engaged accordingly. It is irrelevant, from our present standpoint, that the Roman comedy was indebted to the Athenian; theatrically, *The Lady of Andros* may be taken as the type of this situation. In Terence, as in Shakespeare, the conclusion is legal marriage; so love and legality are united at last.

In Ovid, whose influence on medieval and Renaissance writers was so great that his ideas can never be safely overlooked, legality does not count for much.

For this very reason, since Ovid was far from being a mere Don Juan, a love-relationship imposes for him obligations of its own. And even if Ovid understood these lightly—as matters of good taste and civilized feeling—the love philosophy of the Middle Ages re-interpreted them in depth. When, therefore, Ovid tells his lovers that because their love is not regulated by law, therefore love itself must make the law between them—

fungitur in vobis munere legis amor—[1]

he unintentionally enunciated a principle that came to have an almost religious sanction. For Shakespeare's lovers—although Ovid is not the main reason for it— the love between them *is* the highest law, and the exterior law must eventually conform to it, and not conversely.

In Ovid, infidelities by either partner were permissible. In the medieval tradition, fidelity between lovers was essential, but marriage was irrelevant and sometimes excluded. The ideal Shakespeare presents combined fidelity with marriage. But marriage may have an other than ordinary meaning in Shakespeare. It is rather a symbol of love's permanence—"the marriage of true minds"—than any kind of ceremony. And in the sonnets, where his deepest intuitions are expressed, and where no ceremony is in question, what is being recognized is an indestructible relationship:

As easy might I from myself depart,
As from my soul which in thy breast doth lie:
That is my home of love—   109

---

[1] *Ars Amatoria*, II, 158.

As in the *Phaedrus*, sex is beside the point here. But it is not always so. Spenser is also drawing on the *Phaedrus*—ultimately—for his doctrine of companion souls; and they do become lovers, in the normal romantic sense, on earth. It was possible to have it both ways; and I am inclined to think that Shakespeare did.

In *The Passionate Pilgrim*, he himself tells us of his admiration for Spenser:

> Spenser to me, whose deep conceit is such
> As, passing all conceit, needs no defence.

"Conceit", of course, is being used in a good sense here; and this reference gives Spenser unique importance as a link.[1] He is a poet with whose prolixity it is easy to become impatient; but for our present purpose we have only to regard him as a transmitter of ideas, and in this rôle he is of lively interest. On the one hand, his debt can be traced to the Florentine academicians, and on the other, it is virtually certain that Shakespeare gave sympathetic consideration to his version of their theory of love.

The main points of this theory are conveniently set out in *An Hymne in Honour of Beautie*. It depends on the Platonic belief in pre-existence—as adapted by the Italian Neo-Platonists—and it explains true love as an act of recognition between immortal companions:

> For love is a celestiall harmonie
> Of likely harts composed of starres concent,

[1] Professor A. F. Potts has shown that the subject is even more important than I had suspected; see his *Shakespeare and The Faerie Queene*, 1958.

Which ioyne together in sweete sympathie,
To work each others ioye and true content,
Which they have harbourd since their first descent
Out of their heavenly bowres, where they did see
And knew ech other here belov'd to bee.

If all goes well, something of the harmony of heaven
will be realized upon earth. But it is by no means
certain that the lovers will recognize each other in this
world. They may get entangled with the wrong
partners; and in that case, says Spenser warningly, "It
is not love but a discordant warre". Clearly, all this has
dramatic possibilities; and Shakespeare might have
used them, even if he did not believe the theory in its
Spenserian form. At all events, it will not be frivolous
to enquire if he did, and whether the couples in *A
Midsummer Night's Dream*, for instance, are moved by
such concealed strings.

But whatever conclusion we may come to on this,
Shakespeare's main statement is something more
fundamental. If we press our original question—
"Why, for more than romantic reasons, is the highest
duty of Shakespearean lovers neither to their parents
nor to the law, but to love?"—the answer might be
because love, and nothing else, will lead the soul to
perfection. The Renaissance "Platonists" were agreed
about that, and I suggest it provisionally. But it leaves
many knots to unravel; and they will be impossible to
loosen, unless we take hold of the threads of philosophic
argument at their beginnings in Plato and Plotinus.
Sometimes, it may almost seem as if Shakespeare is
being difficult on purpose, as if he thought rather as
Yeates did:

God loves dim ways of glint and gleam;
To please him well my verse must be
A dyed and figured mystery;
Thought hid in thought, dream hid in dream.

It should cause no surprise to us if Shakespeare held the same opinion. The Renaissance was an age of mysterious philosophies; and it delighted to express them in a veiled way, so that they should be both published and not published, in Pico della Mirandola's phrase, "*editos esse et non editos*".[1] At least it would be unwise to assume, in studying Shakespeare, that what shows on the surface is all that he intends. But although his thought may be difficult to explore, I am convinced that it was not confused: he himself knew clearly what he meant, and it should not be impossible for us to find out what it was.

[1] *De hominis dignitate*, ed. Garin, p. 156.

Chapter II

THE CLASSICAL BACKGROUND

The Symposium

IT may be thought superfluous—if not rude—to quote from anything so familiar as the *Symposium*. Writers on Renaissance philosophy usually take Plato and Plotinus as read, and plunge straight into the fifteenth century. This is proper in a general work; but in a book that aims to trace the vicissitudes of one line of thought, it seems to me that the point of origin ought to be included. Nearly all Renaissance theorizing on love and beauty stems from the two great speeches of Socrates, in the *Symposium* and the *Phaedrus*. Besides the legitimate development of Plato's thought on these subjects, a great deal has been fathered on to him that he never said, and would possibly have disapproved of; and this surely makes it excusable to reiterate his principal points.

During their preliminary conversations, as Socrates relates them, Diotima says to him:

"What *is* this activity called Love? Can you tell me that, Socrates?"

"If I could, my dear Diotima," I retorted, "I shouldn't be so much amazed at *your* grasp of the subject; and I shouldn't be coming to you to learn the answer to that very question."

"Well, I'll tell you, then," she said; "to love is to

15

bring forth upon the beautiful, both in body and in soul."[1]

This definition raises more questions than it answers. To bring forth upon a beautiful body is simple enough; but both speakers look on the begetting of children as an unphilosophical activity, and so Diotima proceeds to explain the second kind of love:

> But those whose procreancy is of the spirit rather than of the flesh—and they are not unknown, Socrates—conceive and bear the things of the spirit. And what are they? you ask. Wisdom and all her sister virtues: it is the office of every poet to beget them, and of every artist whom we may call creative.

This inevitably calls for some definition of beauty. What is it that the soul is to unite with in order to become fruitful? The answer leads us insensibly to the idea that love is also a quest for beauty, or is the cause of one; and this quest is described as an ascent, or expansion of the understanding, leading to a revelation:

> "And now, Socrates, there bursts upon him that wondrous vision which is the very soul of the beauty he has toiled so long for. It is an everlasting loveliness which neither comes nor goes, which neither flowers nor fades; for such beauty is the same on every hand, the same then as now, here as there, this way as that way, the same to every worshipper as it is to every other.
>
> "Nor will his vision of the beautiful take the form of a face, or of hands, or of anything that is of the flesh; it will be neither words, nor knowledge, nor a

[1] Translation by Michael Joyce, in Plato, *Five Dialogues*, Everyman's Library, ed. 1938.

something that exists in something else such as a living creature, or the earth, or the heavens, or anything that is, but subsisting of itself and by itself in an eternal oneness; while every lovely thing partakes of it in such sort that however much the parts may wax and wane, it will be neither more nor less, but still the same inviolable whole.

". . . And this is the way, the only way, he must approach, or be led towards, the sanctuary of Love: starting from individual beauties, the quest of the universal beauty must find him ever mounting the heavenly ladder, stepping from rung to rung, that is, from one to two, and from two to *every* lovely body; from bodily beauty to the beauty of institutions; from institutions to learning, and from learning in general to the special lore that pertains to nothing but the beautiful itself: until at last he comes to know what beauty is.

"And if, my dear Socrates," Diotima went on, "Man's life is ever worth the living, it is when he has attained to the vision of the very soul of beauty.

. . . "And remember," she said, "that it is when he looks upon beauty's visible presentment, and only then, that a man will be quickened with the true, and not the seeming, virtue—for it is virtue's self that quickens him, not virtue's semblance. And when he has brought forth and reared this perfect virtue, he shall be called the friend of God: and if ever it is given to man to put on immortality, it shall be given to him.

"This, Phaedrus — this, gentlemen — was the doctrine of Diotima. I was convinced: and in that conviction I try to bring others to the same creed, and to convince them that, if we are to make this gift our own, love will help our mortal nature more than all the world. And this is why I say that every man of us should worship the god of Love; and this is why I cultivate and worship all the elements of Love myself, and bid others do the same; and all my life I shall pay the power and the might of Love such homage as I can. So you may call this my eulogy of Love, Phaedrus, if you choose; if not, well, call it what you like."

Few passages in literature have stirred the imagination of Europe more deeply than this, and the Renaissance was particularly responsive to it. The soul is presented, here, as the feminine partner in a supremely fruitful union with beauty; but the concept of beauty has been so expanded as to be almost indistinguishable from essence or spirit. Although Plato was not primarily a mystic, his conclusion, if expressed in those terms, is one of the perennial statements of mysticism. "It is as if man and woman embraced and a conception took place",[1] is how a Chinese sage describes the immaculate birth that follows the opening of "the golden flower". And whatever it may mean, this cannot be dismissed as the word-spinning of a philosopher-stylist, because a comparable experience has often been recorded independently.

There are a few statements that last out the centuries —"That thou art", "God is Love", "Know thyself"— which are not fully understandable, and yet have a validity at some level that makes them impregnable. Their very function may be to "tease us out of thought" into vision. And among these—its subsequent history justifies the claim—must be placed the great Socratic assertion: *The soul that is united with perfect beauty*

[1] *The Secret of the Golden Flower*, translated by Richard Wilhelm commentary by C. G. Jung, p. 34.

brings forth perfect virtue. But this affirmation was not *End.* simply re-iterated in succeeding centuries, it was re-interpreted, and it is for this that we must watch.

Although many aspects of love are discussed in the *Symposium*, the one that is chiefly emphasized is creativeness. In the first speech, love is said to be the power that emerges from chaos to establish order in the material universe. Then its influence on plants and animals is touched upon. The healthful harmony of all living bodies is ascribed to it. And we are led gradually to the conclusion that the whole unfolding of existence is love's work—rising to art, science, philosophy, and culminating in perfect virtue. There are some philosophers who look on all this as an unfortunate lapse on Plato's part, and hasten to re-inter themselves in his less lyrical productions; but the theme has never ceased to inspire the poets, and never more pervasively than in the age of Shakespeare. The pith of it is presented in the lines of Ben Jonson:

> So love emergent out of chaos brought
>   The world to light!
> And gently moving on the waters, wrought
> All form to sight!
>   Love's appetite
> Did beauty first excite:
> And left imprinted in the air
>   Those signatures of good and fair,
> Which since have flowed, flowed forth upon the
>   sense,
> To wonder first, and then to excellence,
> By virtue of divine intelligence![1]

[1] *Love's Triumph through Callipolis.*

The Phaedrus

The second supporting pillar of Renaissance theory is the *Phaedrus*. Creativeness is not the only thing that is suggested by the doctrine of the ascent: and this dialogue presents the equally important aspect of discovery. In Plato's view, the best that can be created in the world of time will never be more than material copies of spiritual ideas: these originals are not subject to making and unmaking; and, therefore, the only possible activity with regard to them is not to shape, but to unveil. This can be done; because, as Plato believes, the soul belongs to the spiritual world by its nature, and so to unveil is ultimately to remember.

Love is still represented as the moving power in this; but in the *Phaedrus*, the stress falls on love as a means to revelation. With Renaissance philosophy as the end in view, this idea is perhaps even more important than that of creativity. By the sixteenth century, the *Phaedrus* had not only been translated into Latin, but also—for the convenience of the ladies—into Italian[1]; and Ficino's original preface was reprinted in this edition, to encourage the fair reader, which is an interesting tribute to her vital rôle in the redevelopment of "Platonism".

Revelation, inspiration, vision in the mystic sense—it is all a way of knowing something without having thought it out. No one respected reason more than Socrates, and no one was more sure that there is a

[1] *Il Fedro, overo il diologo del Bello di Platone*, tradotto in lingua Toscana, per Felice Figliucci, Senese. Roma, 1544. Con privilegio del Sommo Pontefice per anni X. "Alle Donne veramente nobili & virtuosi."

sphere of knowledge that reason cannot attain. When his arguments reach their highest point, they become visions. But the use of reason is what makes people sane, to dispense with it is to be a lunatic; and so the highest kind of knowledge is reserved for the divinely mad.

> Lovers and madmen have such seething brains,
> Such shaping fantasies, that apprehend
> More than cool reason ever comprehends.
> The lunatic, the lover, and the poet
> Are of imagination all compact.   *M.N.D.* V. i

Shakespeare presumably took this notion from the *Phaedrus*, adding the obvious point that there is a lower as well as a higher kind of irrationality.

But to sensible people, all this begs a question. If it is impossible for a lover to be reasonable, would it not be better to restrain all loving lunatics, or at least to discourage them, and to regulate human relationships in a calm and logical way? So rational a man as Socrates is predisposed to think so, and he makes a cogent speech to this effect. The discussion seems to be over; and he is about to leave the shady tree under which he and Phaedrus have been sitting, when he has a warning of conscience:

> And I thought that I heard a voice saying in my ear that I had been guilty of impiety, and that I must not go away until I had made an atonement.[1]

After all, he points out, Love is a god, and therefore he cannot be evil. But the previous speeches took no account of this; and so Socrates proceeds to explain the madness of the lover as a form of true inspiration, like

[1] Jowett's translation in *The Dialogues of Plato*, vol. I, Oxford, 1892, p. 447.

that of the prophet and the poet: all of these may appear to be mad; but what they really possess is a sacred gift, which is indispensable to the revelation of divine things:

> For the prophetess at Delphi, as you are well aware, and the priestesses of Dodona, have in their moments of madness done great and glorious service to the men and cities of Greece, but little or none in their sober mood.

Something similar is true of the poets. "But he who, having no touch of the Muses' madness in his soul, comes to the door and thinks that he will get into the temple by the help of art—he, I say, and his poetry are not admitted."[1]

Reasonable people, in fact, have strict limitations, but beyond them is a glorious company of inspired lunatics, to which true lovers also belong. And just as the prophet and the poet had each a special kind of revelation, so has the lover. This Socrates proceeds to analyse, and it turns out to be the best. He shows that it leads the soul to the recollection of its true nature; and that is to say, that it leads to heaven; for the soul is intrinsically divine, but from falling into embodiment on earth it has lost its wings, and forgotten its reality.

It finds, however, on earth, copies or imperfect images of the things of heaven—beauty, wisdom, goodness, and the like—which it once knew in their perfection. "But few only retain an adequate remembrance of them; and they, when they behold here any image of that other world, are rapt in amazement; but they are ignorant of what this rapture means, because

[1] *Op cit.*, p. 451.

they do not clearly perceive."[1] The most vivid and easy to recall of the divine realities is beauty; and beauty, therefore, plays a special part in the re-awakening of the soul to heavenly things.

But of beauty, I repeat again that we saw her there shining in company with the celestial forms; and coming to earth we find her here too, shining in clearness through the clearest aperture of sense. For sight is the most piercing of our bodily senses; though not by that is wisdom seen. . . . But this is the privilege of beauty, that being the loveliest she is also the most palpable to sight.

Now he who is not newly initiated or who has become corrupted, does not easily rise out of this world to the sight of the true beauty in the other; he looks only at her earthly namesake, and instead of being awed at the sight of her, he is given over to pleasure, and like a brutish beast he rushes on to enjoy and beget. . . .

But he whose initiation is recent, and who has been the spectator of many glories in the other world, is amazed when he sees anyone having a godlike face or form, which is the expression of divine beauty; and at first a shudder runs through him, and again the old awe steals over him; and then looking upon the face of his beloved as of a god he reverences him, and if he were not afraid of being thought a downright madman, he would sacrifice to his beloved as to the image of a god."[2]

So however little the lover may be aware of the fact, what he is really in love with is the celestial reality, faintly shining through the earthly form. He will never be fully satisfied until this is perceived and

[1] *Op. cit.*, p. 456.   [2] *Op. cit.*, p. 457.

23

known; but from the moment he truly loves, his soul will begin to recover its lost wings. "He would like to fly away, but he cannot; he is like a bird fluttering and looking upward and careless of the world below; and he is therefore thought to be mad." And this, Socrates explains, accounts for Love's poetic name:

> Mortals call him fluttering Love,
> But the Immortals call him winged one,
> Because the growing of wings is a necessity to him.[1]

It has now become abundantly clear that the kind of love Socrates is leading up to is one that has in it no carnality at all: its real purpose is to restore the human soul to heaven, by re-awakening the knowledge of its own divinity. Distinctions of sex are therefore irrelevant. The relationship is from soul to soul. And the union envisaged is that subsisting between all pure beings in the spiritual world. It might be noticed here —taking a brief forward glance—that many readers feel rather bewildered, some even offended by the unnatural ring of the line in which Shakespeare gives us the key to his intention in *The Phoenix and the Turtle:*

It was married chastity.

But when we give due weight to Shakespeare's Platonism, there is little doubt that the idea originates in the *Phaedrus*; for chastity between lovers—though in this case not "married"—is the specific condition that Socrates lays down for those who are resolved to take, as it were, the short and steeper path to heaven.

[1] *Op. cit.,* p. 459.

This is clearly what the Phoenix and the Turtle had done. They had been acting on the advice of Socrates, who, having brought his lovers together, thus proceeds:

> After this their happiness depends upon their self-control; if the better elements of the mind which lead to order and philosophy prevail, then they pass their life here in happiness and harmony—masters of themselves and orderly—enslaving the vicious and emancipating the virtuous elements of the soul; and when the end comes, they are light and winged for flight, having conquered in one of the three heavenly or truly Olympian victories; nor can human discipline or divine inspiration confer any greater blessings on man than this.

Such attainment is of necessity for the few. But the love of those who make a moderate concession to their desires, although it cannot fully restore the wings of the soul, is still of vast benefit. When they pass out of the body, they are as yet unwinged, but they are prepared to mount; and this is a lasting good:

> For there is a law that the paths of darkness beneath the earth shall never again be trodden by those who have so much as set their foot on the heavenward road, but that walking hand in hand they shall live a bright and blessed life, and when they recover their wings, recover them together for their love's sake.

The first part of this speech gives us the key to Shakespeare's thought in *The Phoenix and the Turtle*. The second is even more helpful: through failing in perfection, these lovers have gained in dramatic value. Those who achieve the condition of "Two distincts, division none", have made their final exit from the theatre; but the others—so far as I know—are the first pair of companion souls in literature, and thus introduce a theme which, after vicissitudes and alterations, becomes explicit in Spenser and possibly implicit in Shakespeare.

For Plato, the companions were first attracted to each other on earth because they had formerly been in the company of the same god in heaven—there is a spiritual tie between them. This required re-interpretation in the Renaissance; and as there was still a recognized association between the gods and the planets, an astrological explanation of such affinities was natural. Spenser found this already worked out for him by Ficino. And so his immortal companions, although originating in the *Phaedrus*, become "likely harts composed of starres concent". But before passing to the Renaissance, we must bestow a glance on Plotinus.

Plotinus

Plato had affirmed that beyond the world that is in continual flux, there is an ideal world of stable principles. Plotinus—systematizing Platonic philosophy in the light of his own vision, and the thought of six intervening centuries—conceived this higher world as triple: the One, the Universal Mind, and the Universal Soul. This is the Neo-Platonic trinity—a divine cosmos, of which the material world is a reflection or emanation.

The universe is thus conceived at four levels; and each of these is receptive to the one above it and creative of the one beneath. With respect to the material world, therefore, soul is the formative agency; and Spenser is still in this line of thought when he says:

For soule is forme, and doth the bodie make.

But individual souls, when they are immersed in matter, are liable to forget their true nature. And if this happens, their vision of the upper world is lost: looking downward only, they mistake the shadows and reflections of the material world for reality. In this state they are in servitude. They can neither escape from matter nor bring it to order and harmony, until they re-assert their divine selfhood. And Plotinus suggests that two appeals should be made to them: one is to point out the shame of the things they now honour, and the other is to teach or remind them of their lofty race and rank.

As we must restrict our discussion of Plotinus to the aspects of his philosophy that are most relevant to Renaissance literature, we will only consider, here, the rôle which he assigned to Beauty as an awakening power. His argument is not fundamentally different from Plato's, but there is a shift of emphasis that is quite significant for the end we have in view. We have noticed that love's creativeness was stressed in the *Symposium*, and its ecstasy in the *Phaedrus*—both leading to the re-discovery of immortal Beauty. Plotinus, in *Ennead* I, vi—which is indispensable reading for students of Renaissance thought—leads up to the idea of purification as a means to the same end.

Since the soul belongs to the divine world, its beauty is intrinsic; therefore self-discovery and the revelation of the beautiful must be simultaneous events which are mutually implied. This is a point which comes out strongly in Shakespeare, and so its provenance is worth notice. Before he defines the beauty of the soul, Plotinus invites us to consider its opposite. We are to reflect on a seemingly-ugly soul—intemperate and unjust, a slave to passion, divided against itself, beset by fear, and fixing its gaze on the perishable and the base. How did it ever reach this dreadful state? Clearly, its original divinity has been obscured—

> —just as one who wallowed in mire and slime would no longer display the beauty which he had formerly, and would seem to be the mud and slime which clung to him. In this case, he derives his ugliness from the accretion of something of a foreign nature and it will be necessary for him, if he is to be beautiful once more, to wash away his stains and purify himself, so as to become that which he was. If then we say that the soul becomes evil through stooping towards, and mingling and confusing itself with body and matter, we shall be right.   I. vi, 5

The beauty of the soul, then, is not something that is made, like a work of art, but a reality that is revealed. What the ugly soul requires is purification, and then it will shine again with its own light.

> When therefore the soul is purified, she becomes form and reason, altogether incorporeal, intellectual, and wholly of the divine order whence is the fountain of beauty and all that is akin thereto.   I. vi, 6

Purification was, of course, a most important rite in the celebration of the Mysteries, to which Plotinus next refers. The removing of garments was a symbolic action, to imply that the soul must set aside everything that disguises its true nature before it can come to perfect knowledge of itself and of its Source. I think it worth while to bear in mind, in this context, the immense significance that Shakespeare gives to masks, disguises, suits and trappings, and to the need for their ultimate stripping off: it is quite possible that Ficino's translation of Plotinus was known to him; and even if it was not, the tractate on the Beautiful is the original source of some of his ideas. In any case, he could not have failed to be aware, even though indirectly, of the culminating conception to which Plotinus is now leading up:

> Just as those who penetrate into the innermost sanctuaries of the mysteries, after being first purified and divesting themselves of their garments, go forward naked, so must the soul continue, until anyone, passing in his ascent beyond all that is separate from God, by himself alone contemplates God alone, perfect, simple and pure, from whom all things depend, to whom all beings look, and in whom they are, and live, and know. For he is the cause of Being, Life and Intelligence. If, then, anyone beheld him, with what love would he be inspired . . . with what bliss would he be overcome! He that has not yet beheld him may desire him as Good, but, to him that has, it is given to love him as Beauty. I. vi. 7

The One Principle, of which we were previously assured by dialectic, has become the supreme experience. Like Plato, Plotinus makes his approach by logic; but logic will not reach to the end. The ascent of Love, the unveiling of Beauty, and the discovery of the

Self culminate in the experience of union with God:
and I think it would be difficult to over-estimate the
importance that this idea assumed for Renaissance
"Platonists". It is clearly not possible, in this thumb-
nail sketch, to give Plotinus his due; and I will merely
invite my readers to notice how strongly the Renaissance version of the ascent is coloured by the passage
with which these quotations must conclude:

What, then, is the way? What are the means?
How shall a man behold this ineffable beauty which
remains within, deep in its holy sanctuaries, and
proceeds not without where the profane may view it?
He that is able, let him arise and follow into this
inner sanctuary, nor look back towards those
bodily splendours which he formerly admired. For
when we behold the beauties of body we must not
hurl ourselves at them, but know them for images,
vestiges, and shadows, and flee to That of which
they are reflections. For if a man rushes towards
them, seeking to grasp them for Beauty Itself, then
it will be as though he should desire to grasp a
beautiful image mirrored in water, and, like him of
whom the myth tells, should sink beneath the
surface of the stream and disappear. In like manner,
he that reaches out after corporeal beauties, and will
not let them go, will plunge not his body but his
soul into gloomy depths abhorred by intellect, will
remain blind in Hades, and both here and hereafter
will have converse only with shadows.
How truly might someone exhort us: "Let us,
then, fly to our dear country." . . . Our feet will not
take us there, for all they can do is to carry us from
one part of the earth to another. Nor will it avail to
make ready horses for a chariot, or ships on the sea:
all these things we must let go. We must not even

look; but with our eyes all but closed we must exchange our earthly vision for another, and awaken that—a vision which all possess but few use. I. vi. 8

This final sentence was simply appropriated by Castiglione in *The Book of the Courtier*, where Shakespeare undoubtedly read it. But I suspect that he knew more of Plotinus than that. And it may even be that we have an echo of the earlier part of this passage in Rosaline's remark to the King of Navarre in *Love's Labour Lost*. The ladies are all masked, and their lovers are all fooled by their disguises into making love to the wrong partners. Clearly, the point of the scene is that they are taking illusion for reality. And Rosaline says:

O vain petitioner! beg a greater matter;
Thou now request'st but moonshine in the water.
V. ii

That the "greater matter" is the real beauty, in contradistinction to the "images, vestiges, and shadows", is a conclusion to which further analysis of the early plays will lead. But that is to anticipate. We must first notice how the Renaissance received and adapted the idea of the ascent.

Plato and Plotinus, taken in conjunction (no distinction between their systems was then drawn), presented the fifteenth century with an electrifying assertion: the soul is divine by nature, and therefore it is a key, if perfectly known, to the knowledge of the whole; between true lovers, this self-discovery is mutually made, and the fruit of such love is the fullness of virtue.

31

These propositions proved most stimulating to spiritual and aesthetic adventure. They were acceptable to the new religious humanism—indeed, a part of its foundation; and they were found concordant with Christianity, because Ficino at once related them to the words of Christ—"I say unto you, ye are gods; and all of you children of the Most High."

Chapter III

PLATO IN FLORENCE

THE revival of Platonism and Neo-Platonism in the fifteenth century makes a pregnant epoch in European thought; and by the sixteenth century there was nothing—from theology and politics to painting and the theatre—that the ensuing birth of ideas had not to some extent refashioned. This vast picture is beyond our canvas. Our modest aim is to account for the Platonic element—if it be granted that there is one—in Shakespeare's love-plots. And with this end in view, there is not much difficulty about the starting-point: it is the banquet held by the Platonic Academy of Florence on the seventh of November 1474. This commemoration of Plato's birthday was the ostensible occasion of Marsilio Ficino's commentary on the *Symposium*—a work of which the influence on art and literature proved to be immense.

By this date, Ficino had already translated the whole of Plato's works into Latin—translations which were not superseded until the nineteenth century; and he was also deeply versed in the Neo-Platonists—Plotinus, Porphyry and Proclus—all of whom he translated later. His so-called commentary on the *Symposium* is, in fact, a highly original interpretation of it, and taken together with his more ambitious work, the *Theologia Platonica*, it constitutes an independent philosophy.

c

SHAKESPEARE AND PLATONIC BEAUTY

There has been some debate as to whether the doctrines of the Florentine Academy should be called Platonic or Neo-Platonic: it scarcely matters, since either term is inexact. No distinction was drawn in the Renaissance between the two, and to harmonize both of them with Christianity was the avowed aim of Marsilio Ficino. He wished to do with Plato what Aquinas had done with Aristotle; and Marsilianism would seem, by analogy, to be the best name for the result. But whatever we call it, we should bear in mind that the system the Renaissance attributed to Plato, although it was Platonic in a general sense, contained much that Socrates would have found surprising.

Ficino wrote his "commentary" in Latin, and then translated it himself, slightly amended, into Italian. His friend, Girolamo Benivieni, condensed its leading ideas into a somewhat cryptic but celebrated poem, *Canzona dello Amore Celeste et Divino*. And Pico della Mirandola then wrote a further commentary to explain the poem—these were ultimately published together in Benivieni's collected works. Spenser's early hymns derive most of their doctrine and some of their phrasing from Benivieni's *Canzona*; but Spenser was well-read in the background literature of Italian Neo-Platonism, which by his time had grown to be very extensive. Of Shakespeare's sources, Spenser was certainly one; but he, too, had others. And he may have read some of Ficino's then-famous translations of Plato and Plotinus, for there is no reason to suppose that his Latin was not good enough to do so. The prime mover in the sequence was Ficino—the *alter Plato*, as

he was known in Florence—and it is to his ideas that
we must now briefly turn.

Ficino

We cannot be sure that Ficino expressed his whole
thought in his published works. He was no Giordano
Bruno, prepared for martyrdom; the Inquisition was
active; he could not have been unmindful of this, and to
some extent it may have restrained his pen. And yet one
of the chief surprises in the study of Ficino is that a
doctrine fundamentally opposed to Scholastic theology
should have been propagated throughout Christendom
with impunity and success. The old orthodoxy could
not accept the intrinsic divinity of man, but this is
Ficino's basic position. It is also the one essential tenet
of religious humanism, and Ficino proclaims it in the
opening sentence of his famous *Letter to the Human
Race:*

> Know thyself, divine race clothed with a mortal
> garment![1]

To this exhortation, Shakespeare's lines in *Twelfth
Night* sound almost like a response:

> A spirit I am indeed;
> But am in that dimension grossly clad
> Which from the womb I did participate. V. i

In Ficino's letter, we have the central conception, that
of the veiled divinity of man—*divini Solis radium
sempiternum*[2]—which made the new Renaissance synthesis possible; but many have perished in the flames

---

[1] *"Cognosce teipsum, divinum genus mortali veste indutum . . .",*
Collected Works, Basel, 1576, vol. I, p. 659.   [2] *Ibid.*

for saying less. As has been mentioned, however, Ficino was careful to relate it, in the same letter, to an unimpeachable text, "Ye are gods."

An important part of his genius—in view of the times in which he lived—was the gift of successful compromise. Whereas Bruno was rigid, challenging and made enemies, Ficino had troops of friends, and a natural flexibility and charm. Whether from conviction or necessity, therefore, he re-phrased the first principle of Neo-Platonism—fidelity to which played a part in Bruno's downfall—that the universe is boundless in space and time. Orthodoxy insisted on a temporal creation, within special limits, and Ficino, though not without some equivocation, met the demand.

The Neo-Platonic quaternity—the One, the Universal mind, the World Soul, and that shadow or imperfect copy of these, which is the Physical World—was retained as a general scheme. But he altered the terminology to God, the Angelic Mind, the World Soul, and the Body of the World, and describes the creation accordingly:

> The Angelic Mind is the first world that God made; the second is the Soul of the Universe; and the third is the structure that our senses perceive.[1]

Each of these worlds is formless, at first; but it gradually takes shape through the activity of divine love. In Ficino's view, love is therefore the ultimate bond of the cosmos—*nodus perpetuus et copula mundi*—and his account of the creation could be justly described as a

---

[1] For the original text and references, see Appendix II.

spiritual love-story. The theory is in some debt to Plato; but it was Ficino who gave to it a characteristically Renaissance expression.

According to this, in the primal substance of the Angelic Mind, there is an innate love of the divinity whence it came; and so turning towards God, it is illuminated; and cleaving to him, it receives form. Thus the Angelic Mind conceives the Ideas—"those signatures of good and fair"—of all that is to be created. This Marsilian doctrine was not found to be heretical; in fact, it won eminent support; and about a hundred years later we find Cardinal Bellarmino quite at home with it. "God," he affirms, "could not have impressed those numberless forms on created things unless in a most eminent and exalted mode he had kept their ideas or patterns in the depths of his own Being."

But the great importance of Ficino's system to the arts, and in particular to poetry, is his insistence that all creation arises from an act of love. The influence of this idea became so far-reaching that his formulation of it is of historic interest. Referring to the beginning, he says:

That still-formless essence is what we mean by chaos. Its first turning to God is the birth of love; its reception of the divine ray is the nourishing of love; its illumination, which follows, is the growing of love; its cleaving to God is the inrush of love; and its reception of form is love's perfection. This uniting of form with idea the Latins call a world, and the Greeks a cosmos. The grace of the world, when it is thus adorned, is beauty. As soon as love is born, it draws the Angelic Mind to beauty, and a substance that was shapeless becomes fair.

In precisely the same way, the Soul of the Universe is said to turn to the Angelic Mind, and the physical world to the Universal Soul. And thus the Ideas that originate in God are brought to birth in form, according to the capabilities of the substance of each world, by the activity of love. This view of the creation is extremely important, in fact, indispensable to an understanding of Renaissance thought. After describing it in detail, Ficino concludes:

> Finally, in all worlds, there is love within chaos. Love precedes every world; it awakens what is sleeping, lightens what is obscure, gives life to the dead, form to the formless, and bestows perfection on imperfect things.

So, in the *Commentary*, Ficino formulated the characteristic Renaissance belief in the creative power and absolute supremacy of love. Without this Marsilian background, one of Spenser's noblest stanzas could not have been conceived:

> Love, lift me up upon thy golden wings
> From this base world unto thy heavens hight,
> Where I may see those admirable things
> Which there thou workest by thy soveraine might,
> Farre above feeble reach of earthly sight,
> That I thereof an heavenly Hymne may sing
> Unto the God of Love, high heavens King.

In heaven, love reigns. And, by analogy, it is the only rightful sovereign of the human soul, for man is conceived as a cosmos in miniature. When we come to Shakespeare, we find it a basic principle with him that when the "crown and hearted throne" are not yielded to love, there has been a usurpation. And it follows in strict logic, from the Marsilian premises, that "Chaos is come again."

As we noticed, the grace or attractive power of the ideal world, as it first appears in the Angelic Mind, is beauty. This beauty, of course, originates in God; and it is by God's absolute beauty that love is said to be stirred in the very beginning. Once again, the process is repeated as we descend the universal scale; so that in every world love is awakened by the beauty of the world above. Considered in this way, love becomes an ascent, a longing for the ideal order and the pure Spirit from which it came. This leads to another conception of great importance in Renaissance art—that the whole creation is drawn to God by the attractive power of beauty. As usual, the influential statement was made by Ficino:

This divine quality of beauty stirs desire for itself in all things: and that is love. The world that was originally drawn out of God is thus drawn back to God; there is a continual attraction between them—from God to the world and from the world to God—moving as it were in a circle. This circle may be said to display three qualities: beginning in God, it is beauty; passing into the world, it is love; and returning to unite the creation with the Creator, it is pure delight. Love, therefore, begins in beauty and ends in pure delight. . . . God is the beauty that all things desire: by this their longing was kindled, and in the possession of it they will be content. Here the ardour of all lovers comes to rest, not because it is spent, but because it is fulfilled.

39

A great deal stems from this passage. For one thing, the special meaning that Renaissance artists frequently imply in their rendering of the *Three Graces*.[1] On the medal of Pico della Mirandola, for example, the Graces represent Ficino's triad—beauty, love, and the ultimate joy, *Pulchritudo*, *Amor*, *Voluptas*; and at the same time they are the circle of eternity—out-flow from, conversion towards, and return into the divine, *emanatio*, *raptio*, *remeatio*; sometimes the central, that is the "converting" Grace is characterized as Chastity, as in Botticelli's so-called *Primavera*; but wherever Marsilian thought has been at work, the Graces become a symbol of this triple heart-beat of the universe.

In Spenser—even in his later hymns, which are less theologically adventurous than his early ones—it is still the attractive power of beauty which awakens "celestiall desyre", and so lifts the soul to God—

Th'Eternall Fountaine of that heavenly Beauty.

I hope to show later that the same recall to heaven is implicit in Shakespeare; and that in his usage, true love-sight—corresponding to the converting Grace of *Amor-Castitas*—reveals the heavenly beauty shining through the earthly, as when Romeo exclaims on his first seeing Juliet:

For I ne'er saw true beauty till this night.   I. v

But before we consider the recall to heaven, which is what the Platonic ascent has become in the Renaissance, it is necessary to understand the theory of what precedes it—the descent to earth.

[1] See Edgar Wind, *Pagan Mysteries in the Renaissance*, Faber & Faber, 1958, chapter 3.

In Ficino, the Angelic Mind is the first form of the creation as God intended it to be—perfect. This great design is realized in the lower planes of soul and matter, but in them it is imperfect. It might be said that at the highest level the divine work is achieved, while at the lower it is still in progress. The final outcome may not be uncertain; but there is a resistance, such as a sculptor must encounter in recalcitrant material. But the beauty "here", although blemished, is always a representation of the beauty "there". The debt to Plotinus is evident when Ficino writes:

> And so it is that the same divine countenance shines, as it were, from three mirrors—the Angelic Mind, the Soul of the World, and the Body of the World. In the first, being nearest to God, it is brilliant; in the second it is not so clear; and in the third, which is far removed, it is obscure.

At the close of the passage, in a striking phrase, he calls earthly beauty the third face of God—*il terzo volto di Dio*. But the metaphor of the mirror is not pressed, for something more purposeful than reflection is assumed to be taking place. Creation—or emanation— is continuous, and the lower worlds are united with the higher by a bond of active love:

> Therefore all parts of the universe, being the works of one artist, the members of one organism, similar in essence and in life, are linked in mutual charity. In truth we may say that love is for ever the knot and binding of the world, its fixed support, and its indestructible foundation.

This was fine theology for an age that found its highest

expression in artistic creation. And having established the scheme of the universe, Ficino turns to man.

In his view, complete man—spirit, soul and body—has correspondences in himself with all worlds, and potential consciousness in each, culminating in the realization of his divinity. This clearly invites, indeed it requires, a theory of man's origin correspondent with that of the three worlds. To frame this, in Ficino's age, was a delicate task; and considering the perils of theological originality, he performed it with astonishing courage and success: by success, I do not imply a judgement on its validity, but that it did not rouse the Inquisition to move against its author, and that for nearly two centuries it was accepted in principle by many brilliant minds.

According to the medieval orthodoxy, God creates a soul, *ex nihilo*, whenever a conception takes place. But theologians were well aware that there are difficulties in this proposition: it implies, either that every conception is the will of God, or else that God creates a soul even when the occasion for doing so is contrary to his will—and neither alternative is easily acceptable. Classical Platonism and Neo-Platonism explained the soul-body relationship by the doctrine of reincarnation, according to which the returning soul found a body and environment suited to its need and merit. And this idea was attractive—but forbidden—to some Renaissance minds. Palmieri[1] was accused, though the charge may have been unfounded, of belief in transmigration. And Michelangelo seems to be reflecting on it in the lines

[1] See N. A. Robb, *Neoplatonism of the Italian Renaissance*, 1935, p. 143.

where he says that every beauty that time steals from his friend's face is treasured in some timeless sphere to be restored to earth—

> *Per riformar di nuovo una figura*
> *C'abbi'l tuo volto angelico e sereno.*

Reincarnation, although it undoubtedly had adherents, was not at that time a doctrine that could be openly espoused. But all Renaissance Neo-Platonists believed —with impunity—in the soul's conscious existence, in higher worlds, before its earthly birth. Spenser elaborates this thought, which he borrowed from Benivieni; and it is one of the characteristic theories of Marsilianism.

According to Ficino, as we have already noticed, the soul proceeds from God, and is intrinsically divine. "Question the pure mind", he writes, "and it will tell you that the soul is not only incorporeal, but also divine":

> *Mens protinus respondebit, non incorporalem esse animam solummodo, sed divinam.*[1]

But on earth, it is clothed—disguised, in fact—by "a mortal garment". His elaboration of this idea came to be widely adopted. In the main, he is re-shaping older theories; but we need not trace his debt in detail here. The God-born spirit-soul cannot, he affirms, be joined to the body directly. There is an intermediate state. Before birth, the soul inhabits a finer body—*corpus aethereum*—which endows it with a double consciousness, divine and natural, and enables it to make contact

---

[1] *Theologia Platonica*, Book I, chapter ii.

with the world below. When the souls come down to earth—through the Milky Way as he quaintly puts it—

—they enfold themselves in a clear and heavenly garment; and invested with this, they put on earthly bodies. The order of nature does not permit the pure soul and the impure body to be joined without this raiment, which, being coarser than the soul, is thought by Platonists to provide a suitable link between them.

In their descent through the spheres, each soul receives certain gifts from the planets. However fanciful this may appear, it is none the less of literary importance. Ficino was an astrologer as well as a scholar, philosopher and priest! In the Christianized scheme, the planets are made to replace, and partly to explain, the classical divinities; and the qualities they bestow on the soul are, of course, ultimately God-given:

In the beginning, God contains the potency of these gifts in himself. He then grants them to the seven gods who move the seven planets—we call them the seven angels who encircle the divine throne; and each of these receives, according to his nature, predominantly one gift.

Uniquely endowed before their incarnation, the souls come to earth with the mission of making their bodies into temples of the spirit, and of imparting to stubborn matter the physical beauties that correspond to their celestial gifts. They work as artists. Some of them—"through unaptnesse in the substance fownd"—have a more difficult task than others; so that although physical appearance and spiritual reality ought to correspond, and it is to be inferred that they finally will, this is not yet to be expected.

44

The Marsilian theory of pre-existence was, in effect, a compromise with the Platonic doctrine of reincarnation. It was soon reflected in English literature; and we need not examine it further in Ficino, because Spenser has made a sufficient statement of it in *An Hymne in Honour of Beautie*.[1] In this form—but not only so— there can be no reasonable doubt that it was familiar to Shakespeare. And I think it may be shown that he was at least in sympathy with its leading ideas, and probably shared them.

In this connection, the points that seem to me of special importance in Spenser's hymne are that the soul is born to do a definite work—to re-shape the world into the likeness of heaven; that it already possesses the heavenly pattern in its own self-nature; that this—the "celestiall ray"—is concealed by the physical form; and that it will only be re-discovered by the insight of true love.

A more likely answer is thus suggested to our problem of why Shakespeare's lovers must, if necessary, defy every kind of authority: it is because love leads man gradually to the discovery—or recovery—of his divine nature:

> But they, which love indeede, looke otherwise,
> With pure regard and spotless true intent,
> Drawing out of the obiect of their eyes
> A more refyned form, which they present
> Unto their mind, voide of all blemishment;
> Which it reducing to her first perfection,
> Beholdeth free from fleshes frayle infection.

---

[1] For the sake of convenient reference, the most relevant stanzas of this *Hymne* are reproduced in Appendix I.

Although these are not original ideas, Spenser produces a general effect rather different from his sources; and his completed picture of romantic love, begun in a former life when the lovers dwelt in ætherial bodies in their "heavenly bowres", is, so far as I know, his own. Other poets took up the idea, however; and they frequently give a false impression that they are drawing directly on Plato. William Drummond, for instance:

> That learned Greecian, who did so excel
> In knowledge passing sense, that he is nam'd
> Of all the after-worlds divine, doth tell,
> That at the time when first our souls are fram'd,
> Ere in these mansions blind they come to dwell,
> They live bright rays of that eternal light,
> And others see, know, love, in heaven's great height,
> Not toil'd with aught to reason doth rebel.
> Most true it is, for straight at the first sight
> My mind me told, that in some other place
> It elsewhere saw the idea of that face,
> And lov'd a love of heavenly pure delight;
> No wonder now I feel so fair a flame,
> Sith I her lov'd ere on this earth she came.[1]

Such romantic developments of the doctrine of pre-existence are Marsilian (Drummond was well-read in Italian), although Spenser's brilliant summing-up puts all later English writers in his debt.

* * *

Within the Renaissance, almost equally important are the two Venuses, symbolizing heavenly and earthly love. It is this conception—after the classical form of it had been re-shaped by Ficino—that underlies the two

[1] *The Poems of William Drummond*, ed. W. C. Ward, 1894, vol. I, p. 27.

great pictures of Botticelli: *The Birth of Venus* and the misleadingly-entitled *Primavera*. The fountain-head of the idea is, of course, the second speech in the *Symposium*, where Pausanias observes:

> Now you will all agree, gentlemen, that without Love there could be no such goddess as Aphrodite. If, then, there were only one goddess of that name, we might suppose that there was only one kind of Love; but since in fact there are two such goddesses there must also be two kinds of Love. No one, I think, will deny that there are two goddesses of that name: one, the elder, sprung from no mother's womb but from the heavens themselves, we call the Uranian, the heavenly Aphrodite; while the younger, daughter of Zeus and Dione, we call Pandermus, the earthly Aphrodite. It follows, then, that Love should be known as earthly or as heavenly according to the goddess in whose company his work is done. And our business, gentlemen—I need hardly say that every god must command our homage—our business at the moment is to define the attributes peculiar to each of these two.

In Spenser, it is the Uranian Aphrodite "Whose beautie filles the heavens with her light"; she is probably also the subject of Botticelli's *Birth of Venus*— in Marsilian terms, the birth of beauty in the Angelic Mind; and that she is sometimes intended to be seen shining through the mortal form of Shakespeare's women is a thesis I will presently defend. But we must not pass from Plato to the sixteenth century without taking account of Ficino. Commenting on the speech of Pausanias, he writes:

> The first Venus, who is in the Angelic Mind, is born of Heaven: she is said to have no mother,

because mother signifies matter to the natural philosophers, and the Angelic Mind has no trace of materiality. The second Venus, who is in the Soul of the World, is called the daughter of Jupiter and Dione. What is meant by Jupiter is the power in the World Soul that moves the visible heavens, and generates all lower forms; and because this is infused into matter, and appears to unite with it, the second Venus is said to have a mother. To sum it up, there are two aspects of Venus: the intelligence in the Angelic Mind, and the generating power of the World Soul. They are both accompanied by love. By innate love, the first is impelled to contemplate the beauty of God, and the second, to re-create this beauty in material forms; the one, having embraced the divine splendour, sheds it on the other, who imparts scintillations of its glory to the Body of the World.

Our mind corresponds to the first Venus; and because of the divine provenance of beauty, the mind is moved to a reverential love when the beauty of a human body is presented to the eyes; while the power of generation in us, which is the second Venus, is stimulated to create a similar form. Love acts in both—in the one, as a desire to contemplate, and in the other to propagate the beautiful. In reality, each love is that of the divine image, and each is pure.

What is it, then, that Pausanias condemns? I will tell you. When the generative love becomes obsessive and blots out that of comtemplation, or when it is performed in some degrading way, or when the beauty of the body is judged superior to that of the soul—then, the true dignity of love is abused.

The continuance of such abuse is said to lead to delusion and enslavement; but Ficino does not dilate on lust, his natural tendency is to look to heaven; and therefore, of the soul ensnared by concupiscence, he says that when it has matured—

—the mind will be moved, by the searchings of its natural light, to recover the divine light; and this attraction is the reality of love.

The Platonic ascent could not have been found so widely acceptable in the fifteenth and sixteenth centuries if it had not been harmonized with theology, and Ficino performed a remarkable feat in doing this to the satisfaction of Catholics and Protestants alike: Benivieni and Spenser, though of opposite allegiance, are at one in the Marsilian idea. And I believe that the same is substantially true of Michelangelo and Shakespeare. For our present limited purpose, the Renaissance form of the ascent is most clearly set out in *The Book of the Courtier*, and so it would be repetitious to follow its details in Ficino. His was the originating mind; but it must suffice, here, to state his conclusions:

The object of love is beyond the body, and the beauty of things lies in their resemblance to a spiritual pattern.

If we delight in bodies, in souls, or in angels, it is not their appearances we love, but the divinity within them—in bodies the shadow, in souls the likeness, and in angels the image of God. Now, therefore, we love God in all things: and finally, we shall love everything in God.

Most views of the heavenly state are tainted with escapism, but Ficino's is notably free from this. The soul does not find its bliss in separation from the sorrowing world, but achieves a love-union with all things, and becomes a universal minister of grace.

Ficino set no limits. Man's destiny is perfection, deification: and when he has risen to become God, as God he loves the world.

Plato, Plotinus and Ficino provided, between them, the new intellectual foundation on which the artists and poets of the Renaissance built. Since Ficino, besides philosophizing himself, translated the other two, it was his work that made the unique qualities of the age attainable; and it has been justly remarked of him that "no writer has been so much plundered with so little acknowledgement". Fortunately for him, the revolutionary nature of his findings does not seem to have been appreciated by the ecclesiastical authorities during his lifetime, for it is hardly possible that they could have wittingly permitted its dissemination. Of his fundamental proposition—that man is a "child of God" truly, in his own self-essence—Saitta writes:

> This concept completely broke through the boundary within which religion had been enclosed by Catholicism, pointing towards a free religion, which is the same thing as liberty of thought. In this way, the Italian Renaissance inspired a process of religious renewal, less wide-spread, but more profound than the Reformation.[1]

That is a claim which it would be out of place to examine here; but it is at least certain that without Ficino's labours the whole climate of sixteenth-century culture would have been much closer to medievalism. The magnitude of his influence cannot be properly assessed until his original works—particularly the *Theologia Platonica* and the *Letters*—are available in

[1] Giuseppe Saitta, *La Filosofia di Marsilio Ficino*, 1923, p. 87.

translation. At present, they are the preserve of a few rather eccentric Latinists; but that is a problem beyond our subject.

Castiglione

All three of these philosophers lack one thing that the artists of the Renaissance, or their audience, could not do without—an emotional interest in the opposite sex. None of them had a wife, nor even—at least, such is my impression—a mistress. The passionate, erotic elements that Dante sublimated in the *Vita Nuova*, and which are characteristic of the medieval philosophy of love, form no part of their experience or their theory. But Renaissance Europe was, of course, still steeped in the traditions and observances of courtly love. They had become somewhat tedious by long repetition: and nothing could have done more to refresh them than a fusion with the thriving young philosophy of Marsilianism. This happened, and the result was a fruitful marriage of ideas.

The thirteenth-century poets returned to fashion. Landino, one of the most scholarly of the Florentine academicians, was soon at work on a Neo-Platonic commentary on Dante. It is likely that Botticelli's illustrations of the *Divina Commedia* were similarly inspired. Palmieri composed a poem of impressive length to correct the Dantean vision of the world to come; but this was judged to be heretical, and remained in manuscript until the nineteenth century. The arbiters of taste and fashion drew up new codes of love; and a host of second-rate writers produced the voluminous literature of the *trattato dello amore*, a genre which, it has been aptly remarked—"exploited the fashionable philosophy much as our modern newspapers exploit psychoanalysis. . . . The Neoplatonic theory of love was attractive, especially in an age in which beauty in all its manifestations was so eagerly pursued."[1] But the theory was changed—and, from the poetic point of view, enriched—by elements that derive from medieval romance.

Before the turn of the century, it might be said that Socrates had joined the ladies; and if we compare his speech in the *Symposium* with that of Bembo, in Castiglione's *Book of the Courtier*, we may almost see him step into the *palazzo*. The social consequences were great. But the lady is not yet triumphant in Castiglione. She is the inspiration for the ascent, but after the first stage of it, merely a useful reminder: she is not a continuing personal presence, like Beatrice, all the way to the empyrean.

Castiglione is not intending to point the upward path of a romantic lover, but of a mature and reflective man. Like Pico della Mirandola, in his commentary on the *Canzona dello Amore*, he describes the ascent in seven stages, which had become the accepted pattern; and as both Spenser and Shakespeare were readers, if not students of *The Book of the Courtier*,[2] these stages are a part of Elizabethan thought. Except for Spenser's *Hymne in Honour of Beautie*, they form the most natural link between Ficino and Shakespeare, and as such they merit careful attention. Castiglione did not number the

---

[1] N. A. Robb, *Neoplatonism of the Italian Renaissance*, 1935, p. 180.
[2] Baldassare Castiglione, *The Book of the Courtier*, translated by Thomas Hoby, 1561, Everyman's Library ed., pp. 315-21.

steps, as Pico's translator did; but he keeps them quite
distinct, and for convenience of reference, I have
inserted the numbering.[1] From the point of view of
our present study, it would not be too much to say
that this *is* the Platonic Ascent.

I

Castiglione's philosopher of love is first delighted by
the sight of beauty in some feminine form; and it is
almost a duty on the part of its fortunate possessor to
reply to this compliment by granting him a kiss. But
like the first kiss in *Romeo and Juliet*, which is related to
it, it is not an ordinary one; it has a sacramental
quality:

> not to stirre him to any dishonest desire, but
> because hee feeleth that the bond is the opening of
> an entrie to the soules, which drawne with a coveting
> the one of the other, poure themselves by turne the
> one into the others bodie, and bee so mingled
> together, that each of them hath two soules. . . .
> For this doe all chaste lovers covet a kisse, as a
> coupling of soules together. . . .
> Whereupon the soule taketh a delite, and with a
> certaine wonder is agast, and yet enjoyeth she it,
> and (as it were) astonied together with the pleasure,
> feeleth the feare and reverence that men accustom-
> ably have towarde holy matters and thinketh her-
> selfe to be in Paradise.

But this initial situation is not without danger: there is a
way down, after the first kiss, as well as up; and even if
descent has been avoided, the lover may now be so

[1] This may be compared with Pico's scheme in Appendix II. See
also, J. B. Fletcher, "Benivieni's Ode to Love and Spenser's Fowre
Hymnes", in *Modern Philology*, vol. viii, 1911.

dependent on her bodily presence that life beomes a torment when she is not there.

II

Release from this is the second step:

—and to enjoy beautie without passion, the Courtier by the helpe of reason must full and wholy call backe againe the coveting of the bodie to beautie alone, and (in what he can) beholde it in it selfe simple and pure, and frame it in his imagination sundered from all matter, and so make it friendly and loving to his soule, and there enjoy it, and have it with him day and night, in every time and place, without mistrust ever to lose it: keeping alwaies fast in minde, that the bodie is a most diverse thing from beautie, and not onely, not encreaseth, but diminisheth the perfection of it.

Her beauty is now part of himself. She has been recreated, in a sense, by his own imagination; and in that form, dwelling ever in his heart, she will not be lost, nor changed by time.

III

He cannot but reflect, however—and this is not accounted an infidelity—that she is not the only lovely creature in the world. His conception of the beautiful is, he now admits, a partial one, and he must extend his view. Although continuing to appreciate the happiness he has—

—the lover shall find another yet farre greater, in case hee will take this love for a stayre (as it were) to climbe up to another farre higher than it. The which he shall bring to passe, if he will goe and consider

54

with himselfe, what a straight bond it is to bee alwaies in the trouble to behold the beautie of one bodie alone. And therefore to come out of this so narrowe a roome, hee shall gather in his thought by little and little so many ornaments, that meddling all beautie together, he shal make an universall conceite, and bring the multitude of them to the unitie of one alone, that is generally spred over all the nature of man. And thus shall he beholde no more the particular beautie of one woman, but an universall, that decketh out all bodies.

What he has now almost grasped, Platonically speaking, is the Idea of Man—a perfect human-being.

IV

At this point, however, if he is a sound Platonist, he will awaken to the fact that he has hitherto been looking in the wrong direction. He has been piecing together his notion of beauty from hints and fragments received through the senses from the material world. In fact, he has been playing a game with shadows; for the substance of beauty, which cast these shadows, is the divine pattern in the Angelic Mind. It is a moment of conversion. He must turn from the copies to the original. He must now close his bodily senses and open the eyes of the mind; for the mind, it will be remembered, corresponds in us to the Heavenly Venus.

When our Courtier therefore shall bee come to this point, although hee may bee called a good and happie lover, in respect of them that be drowned in the miserie of sensuall love, yet will I not have him to set his hart at rest, but boldly proceede farther, following the high way after his guide, that leadeth him to the point of true happiness. And thus in steade of going out of his wit with thought, as he must doe that will consider the bodily beautie, hee may come into his wit, to beholde the beautie that is seene with the eyes of the minde, which then begin to be sharpe and throughly seeing. . . .

Therefore the soule ridde of vices . . . turning her to the beholding of her owne substance, as it were raised out of a most deepe sleepe, openeth the eyes that all men have, and few ocupie, and seeth in her the Angelike beautie partened with [*imparted to*] her, whereof she also partneth with the bodie a feeble shadow.

v

At this first opening of the inner sight to angelic beauty, which comes to it as a messenger from heaven, the soul has a new experience of falling in love. What happened to it before at the earthly level takes place again at the celestial: there is a new kindling of desire, but for union of a different kind.

And therefore burning in this most happie flame, she [*the soul*] ariseth to the noblest part of her which is the understanding, and there no more shadowed with the darke night of earthly matters, seeth the heavenly beautie: but yet doth she not for all that enjoy it altogether perfectly, because she beholdeth it onely in her particular understanding, which can not conceive the passing great universall beautie.

Whereupon not throughly satisfied with this benefit, love giveth unto the soule a greater happinesse. For like as through the particular beautie of one bodie hee guideth her to the universall beautie of all bodies: Even so in the least degree of perfection through particular understanding, hee guideth her to the universall understanding.

The infinite beauty cannot be conceived by a finite mind, but to attain to universal consciousness is to surpass the nature of man. In classical and Marsilian terms, it is a deification: in less daring language, it is to be refined into an angel by the flame of love. "As man he dyes, reviv'd an Angel" is the explanation Pico gives in his commentary on the *Canzona*. And Castiglione had many sources on which he might have drawn, when he continues:

> Thus the soule kindled in the most holy fire of true heavenly love, fleeth to couple her selfe with the nature of Angels, and not onely cleane forsaketh sense, but hath no more neede of the discourse of reason, for being chaunged into an Angell, she understandeth all thinges that may be understood: and without any veil or cloud, she seeth the maine sea of the pure heavenly beautie and receiveth it into her, and enjoyeth the soveraigne happinesse, that can not be comprehended of the senses.

This leads on to the celebrated laudation, and prayer to Love, nearly every thought in which is derived from Ficino. Too long to be quoted in full, and too well known to require to be, it is a brilliant summary of the Renaissance faith in the sovereign purpose of creation.

> What tongue mortall is there then (O most holy love) that can sufficiently prayse thy worthiness? Thou most beautifull, most good, most wise, art derived of the unitie of the heavenly beautie, goodnesse and wisedom, and therin dost thou abide, and unto it through it, (as in a circle) turnest about.
> Thou the most sweete bond of the world, a meane betwixt heavenly and earthly thinges, with a

bountifull temper bendest the high vertues to the government of the lower, and turning backe the mindes of mortall men to their beginning, couplest them with it. . . .

Therefore vouchsafe (Lorde) to harken to our prayers, pour thy selfe into our harts, and with the brightnesse of thy most holy fire lighten our darknesse, and like a trustie guide in this blinde masse shew us the right way: correct the falshood of the senses, and after long wandering in vanitie, give us the right and sound joy.

VII

The seventh state, in the assurance of which the peroration ends, is, of course, union with God: and of this, as of nirvana, everything that might be said is mis-said—except for the affirmation that it is.

* * *

To pursue our enquiry, we must return to earth. Shakespeare had read, and no doubt pondered this; and I hope to show that it was his intention to present a good deal of it in principle. But in the form it is given by Castiglione, it is clearly unsuited to the theatre. What, for instance, has become of the lady? She has vanished. The ascent, after the first kiss, is essentially as Ficino conceived it—"an inner ascent". And the lover could have made the whole of it—and perhaps more easily—in a hermitage.

Shakespeare does not forget that self-discovery is a part of the upward journey; and he gives us the "naked hermitage" in *Love's Labour's Lost*, and a forest of exile elsewhere, as a phase that cannot be left out. But to lose the heroine altogether is dramatically impossible: and—although it is conceivable that she might make a parallel ascent in her own hermitage— is it philosophically necessary, or even right?

Spenser, if no one else, came to his assistance here. Spenser's lovers are companion souls, predestined "to work each others ioy and true content"; and their mutual harmony is a part of the world-harmony. If they fail to achieve this ideal relationship, something of universal value will have been lost; but if they live it —which may be far from easy—then the heavenly pattern will, to that extent, have been re-created on earth, and that is the purpose of love's incarnation.

Spenser did not go quite as far as that, but the adumbration of it would have sufficed for Shakespeare. It was the statement he needed, or so I suggest, to give the philosophic theory a dramatic form. It allowed him all the romance he wished, without loss of spiritual content, all the sad and even-tragic testing, without despair.

Basically, Spenser's position is a return to the relationship of the companions in the *Phaedrus*, who remained happily united, it will be remembered, in this world and in the worlds beyond:

> —for there is a law that the paths of darkness beneath the earth shall never again be trodden by those who have so much as set foot on the heaven-ward road, but that walking hand in hand they shall live a bright and blessed life, and when they recover their wings, recover them together for their love's sake.[1]

To introduce this into the Christianized pattern had

[1] J. Wright's translation.

not been difficult. In the fourth stage, when the inner sight is opened, the soul was said to behold "her owne substance, as it were raised out of a most deepe sleepe", and at the same time to become conscious of the Angelic World. In the medieval tradition, it is love which opens the inner sight to the *seconda bellezza*, or soul-beauty of the beloved. The final consequence, a vision of the substance beyond the shadow, is the same. So Spenser is not inventing, but harmonizing the medieval with the Renaissance pattern when he says:

> For lovers eyes more sharply sighted bee
> Then other mens, and in deare loves delight
> See more than any other eyes can see,
> Through mutuall receipt of beames bright,
> Which carrie privie message to the spright,
> And to their eyes that inmost faire display,
> As plaine as light discovers dawning day.[1]

And so the cloister has become superfluous. Between true lovers, there may be a mutual revelation of the transcendence that no soul can individually possess— "that inmost faire", the Heavenly Venus. And for this reason, Romeo is able to see in Juliet the "true beauty".

Without pre-judging the issue, I think it may be conceded that the Marsilian-Platonist philosophy had reached a point in its development here at which it could have been of use to Shakespeare: it might well have appealed to him as an artist, it had almost attained a form that was suited to the theatre, and it combined the dignity of an ancient descent with the advantage of being in fashion. From the beginning, with Plato, it had been a work of art as well as of philosophy; and in

[1] See Appendix I.

60

Shakespeare's time, it had recently been re-handled by a number of literary artists, each shaping it with a free hand according to his needs and style. I suggest that in the same spirit of creative liberty—which is fully compatible with a belief in its fundamental truth —Shakespeare made it his own. I think we find it in his first plays and in his last; and, as we should expect, that its meaning deepens with its use.

Philosophic judgements lie outside our discussion. But the imaginative value of this representation of the universe is shown by a longevity of some two thousand years: all argument aside, it has the power and the truth of a supreme work of art.

Although torn from a vastly different context, a remark made by one of Boris Pasternak's characters seems to me in place: "But don't you see, this is just the point—what has for centuries raised man above the beast is not the cudgel but an inward music—" The revival, in the fifteenth century, of the Platonist belief in the ascent of Love to imperishable Beauty gave, I would say, "an inward music", not only to the works of Michelangelo and Shakespeare, but to nearly everything that we most value in Renaissance art.

Chapter IV

AN INTRODUCTION TO THE
HEROINE AS THE HEAVENLY VENUS

AS I have already written at length on the early
love-plays—*Love's Labour Lost, The Two Gentlemen of Verona* and *Romeo and Juliet*—I will now take up
only those points in them which show, as it seems to
me, the influence of Platonism on Shakespeare's
conception of the heroine. As in other writers of the
time, the medieval love-lore blended with Platonism in
Shakespeare to their mutual enrichment; but having
discussed the tradition of the Rose elsewhere,[1] I will
leave that aside. There is also a specifically Christian
element in Shakespeare's love-pattern, admirably harmonized with the other two: this is love that will carry
its cross willingly "even to the edge of doom", and by
so doing, become a saving power. The Shakespearean
synthesis draws all these threads together; and so it is
able to trace not only a path from earth to heaven, but
also a way out of hell. At present, however, I will try to
follow particularly the clue of Platonist or Marsilian
thought.

In *Love's Labour's Lost*, the King of Navarre and
three of his lords take an oath to study for three years,
and, during that time, to see no woman. This action is
represented as wrong. Study of that nature, says
Berowne, makes men blind:

[1] See *Shakespeare and the Rose of Love*, 1960.

So, ere you find where light in darkness lies,
Your light grows dark by losing of your eyes.

I. i. 79

The Princess of France also assures the king that "now
his knowledge must prove ignorance"; but she goes
further:

'Tis deadly sin to keep that oath, my lord.

II. i. 105

Why is it so wrong? I suggest that it is because, by the
standards of Shakespeare's Platonism, the king has
vowed to study shadows—books, words, names; and
to exclude realities, which belong to a higher world,
and to which love-sight opens the inner vision. Therefore, Berowne says:

Study me how to please the eye indeed,
By fixing it upon a fairer eye;
Who dazzling so, that eye shall be his heed,
And give him light that it was blinded by.

I. i. 83

If the king gazes on "a fairer eye"—possibly that of his
pre-destined companion in love—he will at length perceive the true beauty. And this will—as in Castiglione's
fourth stage—blind the outer sense and open the
inner. That would be true knowledge, but it is not in
the royal programme.

In spite of his oath, the king is compelled, by his
duty as a sovereign, to receive the Princess of France.
Although he does not realize it at first, she is, I suggest,
his immortal bride, who will be the means of revealing
to him the Celestial Venus. As soon as he sees her, the

63

magic of the eye begins to work; and, for our guidance,
Boyet points this out:

> All senses to that sense did make their repair,
> To feel only looking on fairest of fair;
> Methought all his senses were lock'd in his eye—
>
> II. i. 242

We have already noticed that sight and eyes, by
established tradition, lead to the first initiation into the
higher mysteries of love. And we may therefore
understand that the king has begun to turn from
shadow to reality.

As the princess is to the king, so are her ladies to
his three lords. And Berowne's sonnet to Rosaline
marks the next step in their general conversion. It
affirms that the vow to study must be broken, because—

> Ah, never faith could hold, if not to beauty vow'd!
>
> IV. ii. 110

The idea of beauty is then raised, in the Platonic
manner, to the incorporeal level. The lover who makes
"his book thine eyes" will find not only pleasure, but
knowledge too:

> If knowledge be the mark, to know thee shall
> suffice;
> Well learned is that tongue that well can thee
> commend;
> All ignorant that soul that sees thee without
> wonder—

But even knowledge is not all: in her eyes, there is
"music and sweet fire", and, in the last couplet, a
hint of the vision of the heavenly Venus:

Celestial as thou art, O, pardon love this wrong,
That sings heaven's praise with such an earthly
tongue.

Berowne's sonnet at least shows us that Shakespeare
had the Platonic ascent in mind. In this case, it would
be possible to argue that he was laughing at it, because
he is certainly laughing at all that is still pretentious
and insincere about the lovers; but evidence soon
begins to pile up, continuing to the final plays, that it is
only the falsifications—the "sweet smoke of rhetoric"
that may curl around it—that he makes fun of, and
never the Platonic principle.

If we accept the hypothesis that the universal
Beauty is the revelation that each lover is finally to
receive through the eyes of his eternal sweetheart, we at
once perceive that in the opening lines of the king's
sonnet to the princess, which we are given next, there
is reason as well as rhyme:

So sweet a kiss the golden sun gives not
To those fresh morning drops upon the rose,
As thy eye-beams, when their fresh rays have smote
The night of dew that on my cheeks down flows—
IV. iii. 29

Of all Renaissance-Platonist metaphors, that of the
"ray" proceeding from the divine Beauty is perhaps
the most familiar. And in this sonnet, again, the
concluding couplet points to its source:

O queen of queens! how far dost thou excel,
No thought can think, nor tongue of mortal tell.

With these assumptions in mind, the last sonnet, that
of Longaville, requires no further comment:

A woman I forswore; but I will prove,
Thou being a goddess, I forswore not thee;
My vow was earthly, thou a heavenly love;
Thy grace being gain'd cures all disgrace in me.
IV. iii. 77

In Castiglione's stages, a time comes when the
lover must recognize that the universal Beauty is
reflected in *all* particular embodiments. So far, the
king and his lords each sees his own lady as unique.
But in Berowne's long speech, addressed to all of them,
the universal note is struck: he now says of women's
eyes, in general, that—

They sparkle still the right Promethean fire;
They are the books, the arts, the academes,
That show, contain and nourish all the world—
IV. iii. 353

We are certainly not in the sphere of ordinary love-
making; if this is not nonsense, it must be philosophy;
and there is a Marsilian ring in the concluding lines:

Let us once lose our oaths to find ourselves,
Or else we lose ourselves to keep our oaths.
It is religion to be thus forsworn,
For charity itself fulfils the law,
And who can sever love from charity?

As in Ficino, the climax of the ascent is the finding of
the true self in deity.

The second scene of the fifth act, from line 81 to 471,
turns on the theme of disguise. The undermeaning, I
suggest, is that love-sight must now pierce the disguise
of the body—which is only a garment of the soul in
Marsilianism—and behold the real self. Shakespeare
allegorizes the idea by staging a masquerade. The

lovers have not yet reached Castiglione's fourth stage—the opening of the inner sight—although they are due to do so; and accordingly we see them being fooled by the masks and favours, and making love to the wrong partners, each of them—

Following the signs, woo'd but the sign for she.

V. ii. 469

In consequence, they are once more "forsworn"; because although they have left their books, they are still intent on the beauty of bodies; they continue therefore, as at the opening, to be chasing shadows:

We are again forsworn, in will and error.

V. ii. 471

And Rosaline's remark on this occasion, as I have already pointed out, might have been taken from Plotinus:

O vain petitioner! beg a greater matter;
Thou now request'st but moonshine in the water.

V. ii. 208

To "beg a greater matter"—that is to say, a fuller revelation—is what now remains to be done. As a preliminary to this, we have the death-shock, which is meant to be a vivid reminder of the impermanence of the body. And so we are prepared for the princess's speech to the king, which has nothing to do with romantic love, but points to the final stages of the ascent to perfection:

—go with speed

To some forlorn and naked hermitage,
Remote from all the pleasures of the world;
There stay until the twelve celestial signs
Have brought about the annual reckoning.

If this austere insociable life
Change not your offer made in heat of blood;
If frosts and fasts, hard lodging and thin weeds
Nip not the gaudy blossoms of your love,
But that it bear this trial, and last love;
Then, at the expiration of the year,
Come challenge me, challenge me by these deserts,
And, by this virgin palm now kissing thine,
I will be thine—   V. ii. 817

If we may assume that the princess is intended to be a
symbol of the heavenly Venus throughout the play,
then, at this point, she is her oracle. In his hermitage,
the king is to rise through the refining of love to the
vision of spiritual beauty. This includes self-knowledge,
the soul "turning her to the beholding of her owne
substance, as it were raised out of a most deepe sleepe
—" And beneath the surface meaning of the princess's
promise of union with herself at last, we are to understand, I believe, that ultimate union with the Beautiful,
which, ever since Socrates affirmed it in the *Symposium*,
a long line of philosophers and poets has held to be
love's goal.

It may be thought that I have forced the meaning
here; but even so, I believe it will be granted that I
have not foisted upon Shakespeare any conception
that, considering the context of Renaissance thought,
it would have been unnatural for him to have had. At
this stage, I can scarcely hope that many of my readers
will concede more.

In *The Two Gentlemen of Verona*, we have two pairs
of lovers—Valentine and Silvia, Proteus and Julia. To
Valentine, love-sight comes quickly; but to Proteus it

does not. Proteus is weak and bewildered; and he needs—according to Shakespeare's judgement, which is in contrast to that of most spectators of the play— not punishment, but help. This he is given—by his friend and by his companion soul; and the outcome is a proof of love's redemptive grace.

When Valentine is separated from Silvia, by the sentence of banishment, the shock of it opens his inner sight. We have only to remember the sequence of the ascent, to understand that at this point we are again at Castiglione's fourth step—when the soul wakes and beholds its own substance. In this moment of anguish, Valentine sees beyond the love of body for body, shadow for shadow, to that of soul for soul, and of spiritual union:

> —Silvia is myself: banish'd from her
> Is self from self—
> What light is light, if Silvia be not seen?
> What joy is joy, if Silvia be not by?
> Unless it be to think that she is by
> And feed upon the shadow of perfection. . . .
> She is my essence; and I leave to be,
> If I be not by her fair influence
> Foster'd, illumin'd, cherish'd, kept alive.
>
> III. i. 184

Silvia—like the Princess of France—is both a mortal woman and something more; and it is likely that a Renaissance audience would have seen at once that she is intended to reveal the celestial Love and Beauty. It is not Shakespeare's fault if we miss this point: he does his best—short of ruining the allegory by explaining it outright—to make it clear. And in the next act, we find Silvia at her tower-window, listening to the serenade:

> Who is Silvia? what is she
>   That all our swains commend her?
> Holy, fair, and wise is she;
>   The heaven such grace did lend her,
>
> That she might admired be.
> Is she kind as she is fair?
>   For beauty lives with kindness;
> Love doth to her eyes repair,
>   To help him of his blindness;
> And, being help'd inhabits there.
>
> Then to Silvia let us sing,
>   That Silvia is excelling;
> She excels each mortal thing
>   Upon the dull earth dwelling;
> To her let us garlands bring.
>
> IV. ii. 54

This is a salutation to a goddess. And who should this heavenly Silvia be, but the Uranian Aphrodite? It need not surprise us, then, that Valentine, when alone in the forest—the forest, like the "naked hermitage", symbolizes the solitude in which the final struggle of the ascent is made—prays:

> Repair me with thy presence, Silvia!   V. iv. 11

It is a prayer to be sustained by the power of love and the vision of beauty; and he has no sooner uttered it than she joins him. There follows a melodramatic scene of general reunion, which leads on to the line by which so many commentators have been distressed. Turning to Proteus, who has behaved abominably, Valentine says:

> All that was mine in Silvia I give thee. V. iv. 83

70

When we have understood the dual nature of Silvia, the meaning is obvious. It is not a woman he is offering to give, or to share with his friend, but perfection. No man who has beheld the eternal Beauty could imagine that it was his alone. The point of the line is to show that by the constancy of his friend's love—and of Julia's—Proteus is also able to open the eyes of his soul, and to receive the heavenly vision as a pure gift. And the parallel with Christ's love is, of course, intended.

Turning back to the relationship between Proteus and Julia, we find that he is unfaithful to her, and becomes infatuated by Silvia. Silvia and Julia, in their inmost nature, are one. And so although, as a woman, Silvia rejects him, he is none the less able, when everything comes out right in the last scene, to participate in her divine essence. When she rebuffs him in the fourth act, he begs her for a portrait of herself:

> Vouchsafe me yet your picture for my love,
> The picture that is hanging in your chamber:
> To that I'll speak, to that I'll sigh and weep;
> For since the substance of your perfect self
> Is else devoted, I am but a shadow,
> And to your shadow will I make true love.
>
> IV. ii. 128

It is evident that at this point he is in the condition Castiglione calls "wandering in vanity" due to "the falsehood of the senses"; but that, in a blind way, he is nevertheless groping for "the right and sound joy". But he will not achieve it—in Shakespeare's scheme—without his true companion in love. Therefore, Julia, the rejected, comes now to serve him in the disguise

of a page. With Julia—to whom this is a severe test
—Shakespeare introduces the theme of love as self-
sacrifice, which, because it is willing to carry its cross,
becomes a redemptive power. Her first service is to
go and fetch Silvia's portrait; and when she picks it up,
she says:

> Come, shadow, come, and take this shadow up,
> For 'tis thy rival. O thou senseless form!
> Thou shalt be worshipp'd, kiss'd, lov'd, and adored,
> And, were there sense in his idolatry,
> My substance should be statue in thy stead.
>
> IV. iv. 208

Shakespeare takes great delight in complicating his
shadow-play; but in this case, the meaning is clear
enough. Julia calls herself a shadow here, and Proteus
recently said the same of himself: the reason is that
they both remain shadows until they find their real
selves in one another. The portrait is also said to be a
shadow: and it is likely that Shakespeare knew the
remark of Plotinus, that a bust of himself would be a
shadow of a shadow. What is more important is that
Julia speaks of her "rival" as a shadow: in other words,
rivalry itself is an illusion, existing only in the shadow-
world. There is no rivalry between the two heroines in
their inner nature; in spirit, they are both the Heavenly
Venus. We may, if we like, distinguish between them
in so far as Silvia is relatively static, and so represents
beauty, while Julia is active, personifying love—two
aspects, but one reality.

The final lines of the play, therefore, with the
prospect that all four will be united in harmony, point

to a state, or a consciousness that is beyond the illusory world:

> That done, our day of marriage shall be yours;
> One feast, one house, one mutual happiness.

This may still be Verona, but what of it? "Heaven", as Romeo is soon to tell us, "is here, where Juliet lives". In other words, wherever the true Beauty is revealed is paradise ("Oh! Wilderness were Paradise enow!") and these four lovers have had that revelation, first in each other and then in themselves.

All the talk of eyes and portraits and shadows and substance has been dismissed by some critics as merely "conceits"; but this is to ignore the fact that the use Shakespeare makes of such "conceits" is not occasional and decorative, but frequent and systematic. His portraits form a series. Those that are painted with a brush on canvas are very shadowy; something nearer to truth is drawn by the eye upon the heart, so sharing the soul's permanence, as in the twenty-fourth sonnet:

> Mine eye hath played the painter and hath stelled
> Thy beauty's form in tables of my heart.

This is not yet true vision, but corresponds to Castiglione's second step, at which the lover was told to recreate the beauty of his lady "in his imagination sundered from all matter, and so make it friendly and loving to his soule. . . ". Shakespeare is not following *The Courtier* exactly, but the sonnet shows its influence as he continues:

> Mine eyes have drawn thy shape, and thine for me
> Are windows to my breast, where-through the sun
> Delights to peep, to gaze therein on thee.

These are not "far-fetched conceits", but part of a progress, as in Spenser, towards a mutual revelation of the "inmost faire". Shakespeare has his own version of the ascent, or pilgrimage, and I see no reason why it should have been less meaningful to him than the original was to Socrates. If he were not serious about the principle, why should he return to it in play after play? Why for instance do we find, some ten years later, in the very different atmosphere of *Troilus and Cressida*, that Achilles is still patiently explaining Castiglione to Ulysses?

> For speculation turns not to itself,
> Till it hath travell'd and is mirror'd there
> Where it may see itself.   III. iii

Many people in Shakespeare's audience would have read *The Book of the Courtier*, and recognized the allusion. When speculation "hath travell'd", it is ready to turn on itself. And when it does so with full effect, the inner eyes will open and "the Angelike beautie" be perceived. Love-sight reveals the same reality in the beloved, and that is what Romeo sees in Juliet—the "bright angel", the "winged messenger from heaven", "true beauty". I therefore suggest that the thought-structure on which the whole position rests is the "Platonism" of Ficino: this may fairly be described as religious humanism.

Anyone who will steep himself in the early comedies must come, I think, to feel that the floating gossamer, the fluttering leaf, the shimmering surface are intimations of something more. *Love's Labour's Lost* leaves

74

an audience thoughtful, and it is meant to do that. *The Two Gentlemen of Verona* has left many critics indignant; but this was clearly not intended, and I believe that their annoyance is due wholly to the fact that they have missed the point. But if we grant that there is a point in Valentine's notorious line, an undermeaning that would make it worthy of Shakespeare, then it implies an elaborate philosophy. If so much is conceded, even as an hypothesis, and we reconsider the whole play with this in mind, we uncover, without the least wresting of the evidence, an allegory that is both consistent and profound.

The seed thoughts of this have various origins; but if Silvia is a symbol of the eternal Beauty—glimpsed in the scene where she is serenaded, and revealed at the end of the play—then the source of this idea is obviously Neo-Platonist; and I do not think there is any other theory that provides a satisfactory explanation of the fifth act.

Although there is every reason to suppose that Shakespeare's Latin[1] was good enough for him to have read, or dipped into, Ficino's translations of Plato and Plotinus, this does not have to be assumed. Castiglione, Spenser and the conversation of his perhaps-more-learned friends could have provided him with everything that it was essential to know of a philosophy that was then in fashion.

It began with Socrates. But the details of the ascent are as varied as his commentators, and Shakespeare's favourite metaphor—it was also Dante's—is that of a

[1] For Shakespeare's Latin, see T. W. Baldwin, *William Shakspere's Small Latine and Lesse Greeke*, University of Illinois Press, 1944.

pilgrimage. This does not change the principle: a progress, by love, will, and effort, to reality.

We have seen that Castiglione's seven stages—which can also be traced in Spenser—provide a plan for this spiritual journey. Shakespeare would have known of it from both authors. But if he borrows, he transforms: and I believe that a part of the parable of the love-plays is his own distinctive version of the Platonic ascent.

There is, of course, a great deal more; but it would be helpful to a general understanding of them if we could be sure of this single theme. It is quite likely that in attempting to follow it I shall be accused of mistaking cobwebs and dew-drops for Platonic Ideas; but I must accept the risk. Our own tragic century has inclined us to feel that philosophy is only to be found either in text-books or through blood and tears. This is not, however, a necessary, but a conditioned judgement. Shakespeare could say the deepest things with a smile. Had there been a comic parable in the New Testament, it might surely have been the story of Launce and Crab. But there is no irreverence in Shakespeare, only an ability to see the grace of God in unexpected places.

Chapter V

"A MIDSUMMER NIGHT'S DREAM"

A MIDSUMMER NIGHT'S DREAM, in the text we now possess, was not all composed at the same time; it contains both early and mature verse, and so it is likely to contain more than one stratum of ideas. Dover Wilson[1] sees it as a play "written on the threshold of Shakespeare's career", and twice re-handled. He dates the love-plot and most of the lovers' dialogue at 1592, or before; the scenes of the rustics and the fairy plot took their present shape, he thinks, during the winter following the inclement summer of 1594; while the last revision—"to which we owe nearly all the finest poetry"—was made to grace the wedding of the Earl of Southampton to Anne Vernon 1598.

This analysis brings the love-plot very close in time to that of *The Two Gentlemen of Verona*. It is also close to it in structure. In both we have two men—one a faithful lover, the other a "spotted and inconstant man" —in love with the same woman; she is followed by the false lover into a forest, and he, in turn, is followed by his true, but rejected sweetheart; there is conflict in the forest between the men; and finally, after much play on sight, each recognizes his true partner.

In the plotting, there is likeness; but in characterization, a striking contrast. The lovers in the *Dream* are

---

[1] See introduction and notes to the ed. in *The New Shakespeare*, Cambridge, 1949.

relatively commonplace. The theme of love as service, so beautifully illustrated in Julia, is lacking; so is the unshaken constancy and magnanimity of Valentine, and also the unbroken faith between the heroines. Indeed, the ethical pattern is so much cruder that one cannot help wondering if it was also earlier. Chronology is not our present problem, however; and to recapitulate what is certain, it may be said that the love-plot is the earliest element in the play; that this is very nearly contemporary with *The Two Gentlemen of Verona*; and that, in its philosophy, it seems to be less mature.

It was a consideration of Hermia's problem—whether her first duty was to the law or to love—which led to our long enquiry into the foundations of the ethic by which her answer is determined. And I hope I have persuaded some of my readers that Shakespeare's decision in favour of love—not in this play only, but in principle—is a reasoned deduction from certain premises. The most general of these, shared by many of his contemporaries, is that love is "the manifestation in man of the great informing power which brought the universe out of chaos and which now maintains it in order and concord".[1] This alone would justify his standpoint, since it must follow that every betrayal of love is a movement towards disintegration. But I think there is a fair amount of evidence to suggest that he makes the general proposition personal and dramatic by a further assumption, also widely current in his time, that love on earth is a recognition between companion souls, who may at

[1] J. S. Harrison, *Platonism in English Poetry*, New York, 1903, p. 107.

last perceive in one another, if they have true love-sight, the beauty of their divine self-nature. I believe this hypothesis could shed light on a number of problems in the difficult plays of Shakespeare's maturity, and that it will be worth while to test it carefully in his earlier work. I will not, therefore, embark on a general discussion of *A Midsummer Night's Dream*, but consider mainly those aspects of it that would seem to be related to this idea.

Hermia, then, bravely refuses the unloved Demetrius, whom authority would force upon her as a husband. And she tells the duke that she would prefer "withering on the virgin thorn" to marriage—

> Unto his lordship, whose unwished yoke
> My soul consents not to give sovereignty. I. i

Her decision is doubly right. Demetrius, in courting her, is being unfaithful to his own early sweetheart, who is perhaps his predestined partner. And with this desertion, Lysander charges him:

> Demetrius, I'll avouch it to his head,
> Made love to Nedar's daughter, Helena,
> And won her soul; and she, sweet lady, dotes,
> Devoutly dotes, dotes in idolatry,
> Upon this spotted and inconstant man. I. i

If our hypothesis is correct, therefore, we have two pairs of companion souls, as in *The Two Gentlemen of Verona*, who ought "to work each others ioy true content"; and if they do, they will achieve something more than their own happiness; for through them a part of the "celestiall harmony" will be realized on earth. We may notice that a conception of relatedness, not quite the same but comparable, is also brought into the fairy plot; for the discord between their king and queen is reflected in the elements, as Titania explains:

> And this same progeny of evil comes
> From our debate, from our dissension:
> We are their parents and original. II. i

There may be some folklore in this; but what is more to the point is that it fits in with Shakespeare's wider contention—that the soul-state of his characters is objectified in their world, and that love and hate, however personal their expression, are forces that have repercussions on a cosmic scale.

As we have seen, immortal companions do not always recognize each other when they meet on earth. The body is a disguise to the soul. And the elaborate symbolism of masks and disguises in Shakespeare may well have sprung from this primary idea. Since love-sight is supposed to pierce the disguise and reveal true identity, there is a necessary link between self-know-ledge and love, and so we may readily understand the Shakespearean proposition that the way to the one is perfect constancy to the other. But this is far from easy; and therefore,

> The course of true love never did run smooth. I. i

In fact, Shakespeare stages an almost regular series of impediments. To begin with, bewilderment—when "love is a blinded god", and the lovers are pursuing the wrong partners. Then, as soon as they partially recognize each other, to the extent of "a sympathy in choice", the tests of constancy begin. Sometimes one of them is tested alone by the temporary infidelity of

the other; there is opposition of all kinds, and the trial
of separation. This is the stage of which Lysander
speaks:

> Or, if there were a sympathy in choice,
> War, death, or sickness did lay siege to it,
> Making it momentany as a sound,
> Swift as a shadow, short as any dream,
> Brief as the lightning in the collied night,
> That, in a spleen, unfolds both heaven and earth;
> And ere a man hath power to say, "Behold!"
> The jaws of darkness do devour it up:
> So quick bright things come to confusion.   I. i

These lines were probably added at the final revision
of the play, and so carry the more weight as an expression of settled thought. They recall Juliet's in a
situation which, although far more tense, is correspondent:

> Too like the lightning, which doth cease to be
> Ere one can say, "It lightens."   *R.J.* II. ii

It is a period of uncertainty, when true vision is
achieved only in glimpses and flashes. At the mildest,
it may be called love's springtime, having "the uncertain glory of an April day". But always there is
more than mere romance; it is part of an ascent or
pilgrimage, at the culmination of which the uncertain
glory is made lasting. And its trials must not be avoided,
but faced. By this standard, Hermia's reply to Lysander
is exactly right:

> It stands as an edict in destiny:
> Then let us teach our trial patience,
> Because it is a customary cross,
> As due to love as thoughts and dreams and sighs,
> Wishes and tears; poor Fancy's followers.   I. i

This is a revealing little speech; for just as there are
plenty of "Fancy's followers" in all Shakespeare's
love-plays, so there is also a cross in them, and, I would
suggest, a basis of eternal law.

No sooner have Hermia and Lysander decided to
take refuge with his aunt (much might be written of
the importance to lovers, in life and literature, of
wealthy, childless aunts) than Helena enters. They
confide to her the first part of their plan, which is to
meet in the wood that night; and Helena's decision to
betray their flight to Demetrius, a rather feeble piece of
plotting, is merely designed to bring them all to the
wood, where—as in *The Two Gentlemen of Verona*—
the knot of error is to be untied.

It should be noticed that here again there is no real
rivalry between the heroines. Indeed, there is a firm
link between them; for the proposed meeting-place is,
as Hermia says,

> —where often you and I
> Upon faint primrose-beds were wont to lie,
> Emptying our bosoms of their counsel sweet—
>
> I. i

And later their fundamental unity is heavily stressed:

> We, Hermia, like two artificial gods,
> Have with our needles created both one flower,
> Both on one sampler, sitting on one cushion,
> Both warbling of one song, both in one key;
> As if our hands, our sides, voices, and minds
> Had been incorporate. So we grew together,
> Like to a double cherry, seeming parted;
> But yet an union in partition,
> Two lovely berries moulded on one stem:

So, with two seeming bodies, but one heart,
Two of the first, like coats in heraldry,
Due but to one, and crowned with one crest.

III. ii,

So much emphasis on union in partition—especially
the contrast between *two seeming bodies* and *one heart*—
points to the same conclusion that we reached with
regard to Silvia and Julia: rivalry and discord exist only
between shadows, in the world of illusion; and we are
moving towards an inner reality, where harmony is
law.

Lysander's earlier phrase, "sympathy is choice",
recalled Spenser's lines:

But, in your choice of loves, this well advize,
That likest to yourselves ye them select,
The which your forms first sourse may sympathize—

And there is a further Spenserian thought in the
soliloquy with which Helena closes the scene:

Things base and vile, holding no quantity,
Love can transpose to form and dignity.
Love looks not with the eyes, but with the mind—

I. i

If there is no direct influence here, there is at least a
parallel with Spenser's assertion—the Marsilian background of which we have partly traced—that lovers draw
"out of the object of their eyes a more refyned form",
and with his stanza beginning:

For lovers eyes more sharply sighted bee
Then other mens—

It seems to me likely that the influence is direct.
Shakespeare himself has told us of his admiration for

83

Spenser[1]; and since to admire and to appropriate were almost synonymous with him, we might expect him to use Spenserian ideas. In her soliloquy, Helena goes on to what seems to be a contradiction, stressing love's blindness:

> Wings and no eyes figure unheedy haste.

But there is no contradiction when we remember that Shakespearean love is a progressive activity—always there is blindness, partial blindness, and at last clear sight. This is equally Spenserian. And just as the Red Cross Knight is unable to see Una's true beauty until he has climbed the Mount of Vision, so, in Shakespeare, it is only when love-sight is perfected that bodies become transparent and the immortal beauty shines from within. Shakespeare offers many equivalents of the Mount of Vision—the "naked hermitage" of *Love's Labour's Lost*, and numerous variations on the theme of "the life removed". And associated with them is the same idea of constancy—but not simply to romantic love—severely tested.

In *A Midsummer Night's Dream*, constancy is stressed up to a point. But the fact that love-sight is controlled by charms—

> And ere I take this charm from off her sight,
> As I can take it with another herb—   II. i

and not as elsewhere by the hard work of the soul, makes its ethic seem comparatively weak. It might be argued that the first charm produces nothing except "hateful fantasies"; but there are equally cogent objections to this point of view. And even when

[1] *The Passionate Pilgrim*, stan. viii.

Titania, under its influence, perceives a kind of divinity in Bottom, I fancy that she is nearer, in Shakespeare's judgement, to a true vision of him than when she sees him only as an ass. The juice of love-in-idleness is certainly a cause of confusion; but eyes that have been anointed with it do nevertheless see something real behind the mask of mortality. What they see is something love-awakening. And therefore, if the parallel with Spenser is a true one, it ought to be a glimpse of the "inmost faire".

The first mortal on whom the juice is tried, by Puck's mistake, is Lysander; and the first evidence we have of its effect is his exclamation:

Transparent Helena! Nature shows an art
That through thy bosom makes me see thy heart.
                                                    II. ii

And when Demetrius has been likewise anointed, he exclaims:

O Helen, goddess, nymph, perfect, divine!   III. ii

This is meant to make us laugh, of course; but is there anything beyond the joke? If this new insight is nothing but an hallucination, it is curious that the description of it should fit a theory that Shakespeare has taken seriously in other plays. "Transparent" is precisely the word to illustrate it. Lysander has seen through Helena, and what he has seen is something more beautiful than her outward shape: the whole context of Renaissance thought requires the further assumption that what is more beautiful is also more real. So in spite of the confusion the charm makes, it

85

has conferred something on Lysander that is akin to Spenserian love-sight.

Spenser's chief authority on this subject is Benivieni's *Canzona*, and in this a phase of confusion also forms part of the ascent. When lovers see something in each other that no one else can see, Benivieni admits that they are suffering from a kind of hallucination or "sweet error"—

> *Pascesi el cor d'un dolce error—*

and then he proceeds to the Marsilian paradox that the error is truth, or nearly so. What has been revealed is a shimmer of divinity, like sunlight under water, that is neither full reality nor complete illusion:

> *Come raggio di sol sott'acqu'el vede:*
> *Pur non so che divin ch'en lui lampeggia—*[1]

Benivieni and Spenser had no lively sense of humour, and it probably never occurred to either of them that the phase of bewilderment had its comic possibilities. Shakespeare used these to the full, but without ceasing to respect the principle of the gradual awakening of human love to heavenly beauty. There is even a suggestion of it in Oberon's spell:

> Flower of this purple dye,
> Hit with Cupid's archery,
> Sink in apple of his eye.
> When his love he doth espy,
> Let her shine as gloriously
> As the Venus of the sky.   III. ii

These lines were inserted at the last re-handling of the play. Whatever their antecedents may be, their effect

[1] *Canzona dello Amore Celeste et Divino*, lines 130-31.

is to describe the love-charm as a cause of *dolce error:* the error is that of seeing immortal beauty—*un non so che divin*—in the beloved, and there is a good deal of evidence to suggest that Shakespeare believed this to be the truth. In the poetry of another age, "the Venus of the sky" would be merely an ornamental phrase; but in this context it would come so naturally from the background philosophy that it seems likely to refer to the Heavenly Venus.

To appreciate how widely such a pattern of thought was diffused in the Renaissance, I would invite the reader to consider the symbolism of Botticelli's *Primavera*.[1] The theme of the picture is love as the agent of transmutation and revelation. The presiding figure in it is the earthly Venus. On her left, the elemental passion of Zephyr transforms the simple Chloris, *nympha campi felicis*, into Flora—the beauty of the natural world; and on her right, the theme is lifted, through humanity and the Graces, to an implied revelation of the beauty of the divine world. This is accomplished when blind Cupid, hovering above the earthly Venus, looses his arrow at the central, that is, the "converting" Grace—here characterized as *Castitas:* through her purity, sightless Love recovers the celestial vision, because her eyes are turned towards Mercury, the guide of souls, whose staff is touching the clouds which symbolize the veil before the mysteries. It might justly be said of her that

> Love doth to her eyes repair,
> To help him of his blindness.

[1] See Edgar Wind, *op. cit.*, chapter vii.

And when the clouds have been dispersed, what will shine forth, we must suppose, is the ultimate Beauty—"the Venus of the sky". This is possibly the subject of the companion picture, *The Birth of Venus*.

I do not, of course, imply that Shakespeare knew anything of Botticelli, but simply that they are both drawing water from the same well. The union of the king and queen of the fairies is related to the flowering of nature, although in a more fanciful way than that of Zephyr and Chloris; and it is "young Cupid's fiery shaft" aimed "at a fair Vestal" which gives to the juice of love-in-idleness the power to make bodies "transparent" and to show—or so I would suggest—the soul's intrinsic beauty.

*   *   *

As always in Shakespeare, the dark forces make their supreme effort in the third act, when the men attempt to kill each other. The theme in this act is love before sunrise, and I suggest that it is the kind of parable we might expect. When the powers of light are exerted in the fourth act—and this again is standard construction —the gaining of clear sight leads on to a joyous close.

If Shakespeare is seeing his lovers as companion souls, so that only one final pattern of relationships can be absolutely right, then the third act illustrates Spenser's idea of what is to be expected when the wrong partners try to unite—

It is not love, but a discordant warre,
Whose unlike parts amongst themselves do iarre.

And the same hypothesis might account for the determination with which the spurned Helena hounds

Demetrius down. It is undignified, to say the least; but if they are pre-destined for each other, she is right. This is not the only play in which the heroine behaves like the hound of heaven—there is *All's Well that Ends Well*, for instance; and the current theory of pre-existence, of love cradled in "heavenly bowers", that must be found again and realized upon earth, would justify them all. They are surely in need of some justification; for although no one doubts the ability of the female to hunt the male, it is not usually depicted as a virtue. Helena is painfully aware of this, and calls it a scandal on her sex:

We should be wooed and were not made to woo.
II. i

She is none the less determined to follow Demetrius, "and make a heaven of hell", or die in the attempt.

Against all likelihood, she succeeds. And at the close of the fourth act, when the lovers wake at sunrise, their vision restored, the harmony between the four of them reminds us of that which was at last achieved in *The Two Gentlemen of Verona*. Here again we have the theme that rivalry exists only in the phase of illusion—symbolized this time by the moonlit wood—when Theseus exclaims to Lysander and Demetrius:

I know you two are rival enemies.
How comes this gentle concord in the world—?
IV. i

In the earlier play, it was between the women that rivalry might have been expected, here it is chiefly between the men; but there is a similar allegory, I suggest, in both: when the true beauty is rightly apprehended, concord comes to the world. I think Shakespeare is quite serious about this, and he returns to it many times; but if we insist that there is no parable in his plays, we see only the surface of his thoughts.

In *Love's Labour's Lost*, Shakespeare used masks and fancy dress to suggest the appearances that must be transcended before reality, or the revelation of love and beauty, can be known. In *The Two Gentlemen of Verona*, shadows and the portrait are the figures he employed:

> Vouchsafe me yet your picture for my love . . .
> For since the substance of your perfect self
> Is else devoted, I am but a shadow—   IV. ii

In *Romeo and Juliet*, names are the disguise:

> 'Tis but thy name that is my enemy . . .
>   Romeo, doff thy name;
> And for that name, which is no part of thee,
> Take all myself.   II. ii

And in this play, the metaphor is dreams. "Let us recount our dreams," says Demetrius, when he is finally convinced that they have woken up. And it is in the same tone, that Puck speaks the epilogue:

> Think but this, and all is mended,
> That you have but slumbered here,
> While these visions did appear.

To discard the fancy dress, to find the substance in place of the shadow, to doff the name that hides the self, to dream and to wake at sunrise—all these imply the ending of a period of delusion; and the happy outcome is always reached by the constancy of love to its ideal. Surely it will be granted that this may not be unintentional; and it is beyond dispute that the unifying principle is also the leading thought of the "Platonism" of the age. It seems to me, therefore, to be a not unreasonable theory that the allegory of love, in its ascent or pilgrimage to heavenly beauty, is the inner meaning of all these plays.

> THESEUS: Moonshine and Lion are left to bury the dead.
>
> DEMETRIUS: Ay, and Wall too.
>
> LION: No, I assure you, the wall is down that parted their fathers.

Chapter VI

"AS YOU LIKE IT"

UP to this point, I have attempted to trace a single thread in Shakespeare; but the Platonic ascent is only one of several permanent strands in his pattern, and we must now see how it is woven in with others. I have treated these companion themes elsewhere, and it would be confusing to do so again in detail here. Deprived of supporting evidence, some of my assumptions may seem arbitrary; but they have been defended in other work,[1] and I can at least assure the reader that none of them is put forward casually.

In the opening scene of *As You Like It* we meet the hero and the villain; and once again, as Shakespeare often presents this dramatic couple, they are brothers. We may think ahead to *Hamlet* and *The Tempest*—fratricide done or attempted in them both—and remember that one was a tragedy, because even beyond the grave there was no forgiveness, while the other was a triumph, the prologue to a brave new world, because the ancient hate was ended by creative mercy. We have the same allegory here, the same tremendous choice.

Having studied Shakespeare's ethical demonstrations in other plays, the first short scene of *As You Like It* enables us, by analogy, to foretell a great deal of what is to come. One brother, Oliver, is cheating

[1] See *The Shakespearean Ethic*, 1959.

the other, Orlando, of his inheritance; this has been going on for a long time, and a climax has been reached. Orlando claims his rights: Oliver's reaction is to plot his murder. The conflict is clear; our sympathies are enlisted; and if we boldly trust in Shakespeare's fidelity to his own scheme of ethics, we shall know already that one of two things will happen in the fifth act, and that both of them will depend upon Orlando.

If Orlando determines on revenge—which most people, under the circumstances, would call plain justice—the conclusion of the play will be tragedy. The "death-for-death" sequence—so lucidly set out in *Romeo and Juliet*, *Hamlet* and elsewhere—will be the order of events; and both the brothers, and whichever other characters allow themselves to be sucked into the whirlpool, will die. But if Orlando embarks upon a different course, far harder to maintain, but one that will eventually give him the spiritual power to make creative mercy effective, then the end of the play will be total victory. And that does not mean in Shakespeare that the sinning brother will lose his life —which may seem to be the proper fate of an attempting murderer, and would satisfy most dramatists and a majority in every audience; it means that Oliver will be enlightened, and that the principle of brotherhood and love will triumph. Shakespeare is showing us the ethic that could, if it were applied, bring in an age of gold.

It is imperative that we should understand that in the first scene Orlando is being tempted, and that the sequence of events depends on his reaction. Before this test, in conversation with Adam, he tells us the background of the conflict, and concludes:

> This is it, Adam, that grieves me; and the spirit of my father, which I think is within me, begins to mutiny against this servitude. I will no longer endure it, though yet I know no wise remedy how to avoid it.

At this moment Oliver enters. The brothers quarrel; Orlando loses his temper, and takes Oliver by the throat. It seems as if no wise remedy will be found; but at that moment, Adam steps out:

> Sweet masters, be patient: for your father's remembrance, be at accord.

There are a few more hard words, and then Orlando's wrath subsides. He ceases to threaten, and says:

> I will no further offend you than becomes me for my good.

Every touch here follows an established Shakespearean pattern. As an allegorical figure—which in no way precludes vivid individual character—Adam is one of the long line of wise old men in Shakespeare who all give the advice that it is essential to follow in the moment of temptation: "To thine own self be true." If the hero understands that in its deepest meaning, and acts by it, falsity becomes impossible, the test is passed, and the way is open to self-sovereignty and power. If he rejects this advice, there will be insurrection and chaos in his own soul, and these will be objectified in the outer world.

Adam, therefore, belongs to the group of good counsellors (Escalus, Camillo, Gonzalo are other

members of it) whose principle of fidelity to the true
self contains the secret of how "To bind again this
scatter'd corn into one mutual sheaf". The fact that
Orlando listens to him is of great importance allegorically. In Shakespeare, this clue alone is enough to tell
us that he is moving away from tragedy. And when he
says that he will act "as becomes me for my good", we
may understand an absolute good, which will lead to
victory not over the enemy, but over the enmity.
Oliver's reaction is the opposite: he says to Adam:

> Get you with him, you old dog.

His course is thus set for tragedy, in strict accordance
with Shakespeare's rules of construction; and it is
almost inevitable that the next thing he does is to
contrive a plot of murder.

Shakespeare never forgets that no one can be fully
true to himself without self-knowledge; and the degree
to which the characters in any play approach this is
invariably a measure of their virtue. This clue has also
been given to us. During the quarrel, Oliver asks if his
brother knows in whose presence he is, and Orlando
replies:

> Ay, better than him I am before
> knows me.   I. i

It is standard Shakespearean practice to show that the
lower nature cannot understand the higher; as, for
example, in another scene of violence, Romeo says to
Tybalt:

> I see thou know'st me not.   *R.J.* III. i

The point is that Shakespeare always views the hero
who is on the ascending path as moving towards the

condition of "the perfect man", "man new made". He may still have a long way to go; but the mere fact that he is striving to mount increases his self-knowledge, and bestows on him a fuller consciousness than the lower soul can comprehend.

We are now intended to see Orlando as a soul who, with the help of Adam's timely reminder, has passed his first test. But the upward progress of the Shakespearean hero is always associated with constancy to love, culminating in the revelation of divine beauty; and to present this is the allegorical function of the heroine. As I have previously pointed out, the hero's relations with her—good or bad, cherishing or insulting, and, in the extreme, becoming one with her or killing her—are another infallible indication of the ascent or descent of his soul.

In *Love's Labour's Lost* there were four heroines, each distinct in character and looks, but all subsumed under a single symbol, all one allegorical figure, for each was the way of revelation, to her predestined partner, of the transcendent reality of love and beauty.

In *The Two Gentlemen of Verona* there were of course two heroines—as also in *A Midsummer Night's Dream*—and the offer of sharing Silvia applied not to the woman but to the revelation for which she stood. In the present play we again have two heroines. And again we shall find that the hero who completes the ascent, or pilgrimage, by his own effort has the power to bestow what he wins by merit on his undeserving friend or brother. To raise this point is to anticipate, but I do so in order to stress the consistency of Shakespeare's statements of principle and the unfailing rationality of his deductions from them.

We are told something about the heroines before we meet them. And this information is by no means important to the plot alone. The first point that Shakespeare emphasizes is their unity. Having noted the same thing of Silvia and Julia, and remembering that Hermia and Helena, in spite of some discord when they were lost in the forest of shadows, were still

> —like two coats in heraldry,
> Due but to one, and crowned with one crest—
>
> III. ii

we cannot fail to conclude that the same allegory is intended here: as characters they are two; as a symbol, one. Charles says that if Rosalind had accompanied her banished father, Celia would certainly have gone as well:

> —she would have followed her exile, or have died to stay behind her . . . never two ladies loved as they do.
>
> I. i

When we meet Rosalind and Celia in the second scene, we are therefore prepared, by analogies in other plays, to see them at two levels—personal and allegorical. It is the scene in which Orlando is to wrestle with Charles. In intention, the bout is a disguised murder, which Oliver and Charles have planned; but in appearance it is simply one episode in a public display on the lawn before the duke's palace. Celia is the daughter of the usurping duke, and Rosalind that of his banished brother, who is of course the legitimate sovereign.

G   97

Charles has just given a savage demonstration of bone-breaking, and the ladies try to dissuade Orlando from the encounter.

ROSALIND: Young man, have you challenged Charles the wrestler?

ORLANDO: No, fair princess; he is the general challenger: I come but in, as others do, to try with him the strength of my youth.

CELIA: Young gentleman, your spirits are too bold for your years . . . give over this attempt.

Orlando excuses himself for refusing the ladies' request, and adds:

But let your fair eyes and gentle wishes
go with me to my trial.

The romantic side of the story is delightfully done; and this is not diminished in the least by the recognition that Shakespeare is continuing his allegory as well; indeed, it is greatly enhanced and deepened by this further dimension. The Shakespearean hero is always challenged. As his father said of Proteus:

—he cannot be a perfect man,
Not being tried and tutor'd in the world.

Orlando's test is different; but there are many elements in life by which the hero is tried, and Charles represents one: the power of brute strength, that has to be mastered—not destroyed—by something higher; and that something higher is not merely superior force of the same kind, but power of a different quality. From first to last in Shakespeare's work the laws by which the paramount spiritual power may be exerted are set out with consistent lucidity: *the hero must know himself, be true to himself,* and *be constant to the guiding principle of love in his own soul.* In the first scene we saw that Orlando was on the way to self-knowledge; by his acceptance of Adam, we saw that he would be true to it; and now we have the third element in the pattern—the request that love go with him in his trial. In Shakespeare's scheme, brute strength cannot win against this combination of spiritual forces; and for that reason—as well as for the sake of the romantic story—Charles is thrown.

Naturally, the victorious young man is complimented by the ladies—and in this he is being tested still. Having overcome the champion, he might well have been defeated now by pride. But in fact he is tongue-tied. He cannot even thank Rosalind when she takes the chain from her neck and gives it to him, saying, "Wear this for me—". Only when they have left him does he exclaim:

> O poor Orlando! thou art overthrown.

A charming, romantic scene—but it is linked with the most tremendous things that Shakespeare ever found the power to say. With full and clear intention it is related to the terrible moment when Othello casts down the sovereignty of Love and opens his soul to chaos and hell. Orlando is doing the opposite—as every mounting soul in Shakespeare must—yielding to Love the "crown and hearted throne".

There follows a short conversation with Le Beau, from which Orlando learns something of Rosalind's history and present situation; then he is left alone again, and the scene closes with his exclamation:

> But heavenly Rosalind!

"Heavenly"—the adjective is either hyperbole or allegory; and it is important to determine which. All four ladies in *Love's Labour's Lost* had this epithet, or its equivalent, applied to them. The serenade to Silvia was, as has been said, a salutation to a goddess. Juliet, described as "true beauty", made "heaven" where she lived. And the love-charm in *A Midsummer Night's Dream* revealed a divinity in everyone—even in Bottom. The Platonic ascent, as the Renaissance understood it and as Castiglione's steps unequivocally present it, brought exactly this revelation at a certain point—"the soul . . . turning her to the beholding of her owne substance, as it were raised out of a most deepe sleepe, openeth the eyes that all men have, and few occupie, and seeth in her selfe a shining beame of that light, which is the true image of the Angelike beautie partened with her, whereof she also partneth with the bodie a feeble shadow". No one, I think, disputes that Shakespeare read that sentence. What, then, of the celestial quality in his heroines? Either it is a mere conceit, which he never omits; or else the hero and heroine are being satirized in every play; or else it is an allegory of the Platonic beauty.

If it is a conceit, then he was oddly determined to practise what he condemned—"Three-pil'd hyperboles, spruce affectation". Satire in the magical scenes in which the celestial beauty shines most clearly—Silvia in her tower, Juliet on her balcony—is unthinkable. I submit that no other explanation is possible except the one which is, in any case, the most likely: that as a young man Shakespeare was deeply moved by the poetic expression of Platonic beauty—which he

certainly knew of from Castiglione and Spenser
—and that he allegorized it in his plays with full
deliberation.

There is a curious reluctance, however, to admit
that he was capable of intellectual consistency. Mr Eliot
even raises the question, "Did Shakespeare think about
anything at all?" And he concludes that he did not—
he only wrote poetry. To press this line of criticism to
its logical end, would be to ask, "Did Shakespeare use
a planchette?" Perhaps so, but if he did, it was guided
by some other mind; for a part of his poetry—to take
a solitary instance of the intellect behind it—consists
of speeches composed in strict accordance with the
rules of Ciceronian rhetoric.[1] Cicero was a barrister,
and no one can apply his rules who has not schooled
himself to make a logical analysis of his material—in
fine, to thinking hard and clear.

*   *   *

In the third scene, Duke Frederick, the usurper,
banishes Rosalind. His sudden flame of fury reminds
us of Leontes. Such outbursts in Shakespeare's
characters are not provoked by sexual jealousy alone;
they are symptoms of the kind of madness that he
always associates with evil, and they signify a usurpation by the passions of the lordship of the soul. Every
tyrant in Shakespeare is inwardly in such bondage:
and his tyranny ends with his own liberation.

Duke Frederick is travelling the road that all
Shakespeare's tragic heroes take. He has lost his own

[1] For Ciceronian rhetoric in Shakespeare, see T. W. Baldwin,
William Shakspere's Small Latine and Lesse Greeke, University of
Illinois Press, 1944, vol. II.

self-sovereignty, and this is symbolized by his outward act of usurpation and the banishment of the legitimate duke, for it must not be forgotten that Shakespeare believed that true princes rule by divine grace. The next step in the tragic path is the casting out of love, symbolized by the heroine; and therefore Rosalind is banished, on pain of death. When she protests her innocence, Frederick answers:

> Thou art thy father's daughter; there's
> enough   I. iii

True rulership and love go together in Shakespeare; and the consequence of denying them is always the same. When the hero commits the tragic crime, he is shown to be striking at the best thing in his own life— ultimately, his crime is against himself. So, because he banishes Rosalind, Frederick loses his own daughter. Celia has already warned him of this, saying that she and Rosalind were "like Juno's swans . . . inseparable". And as soon as the girls are alone together, she says:

> —know'st thou not, the duke
> Hath banished me, his daughter?

Every point here has its allegorical parallel in other plays. The inseparability of Juno's swans is another simile, like the "two coats in heraldry . . . crowned with one crest", to show that there is a transcendent quality by which the heroines are made one. Their girlhood friendship is irrelevant to this: Silvia and Julia had never met, and they had some reason to be rivals; but they were united, before they had seen each other, by a shared ideal; and they were embraced in a single higher reality—"the Angelike beautie", Castiglione calls it, or in Spenser's phrase, "the inmost faire".

Frederick has now betrayed both himself and others —when a Shakespearean character is false to himself, he cannot be true to any man; and he has banished Love and Beauty from his world. This is the road back to chaos—within and without; and however tragedy may be defined by other authorities, this is tragedy for Shakespeare. Frederick is turning his court into hell; and to be dismissed from it is to go, in Celia's words:

> To liberty, and not to banishment.   I. iii

*   *   *

Finding that his brother is determined to murder him, Orlando, in company with Adam, also leaves his home. All the good characters have now been dispossessed by the bad ones; and they will soon come together in the forest of Arden, under the leadership of the dethroned duke. Why is it that neither Orlando nor the duke ever considers striking a blow in his own defence? The time-honoured means of righting such wrongs as theirs is force of arms; and every audience would approve it. It cannot be replied that Shakespeare is following his source, because this is his most notable divergence from it; in the original story, the usurper is defeated in battle.[1]

In re-shaping the story at this point, Shakespeare makes it conform to a well-established pattern of his own. This pattern is basic; and if we do not see it here, we shall be in danger of missing some of his most profound intentions in other plays. One of Shakes-

[1] Thomas Lodge, *Rosalynde, Euphues' Golden Legacie*, 1590.

peare's cardinal statements is that there is an effective alternative to revenge, and that unless it is employed, the pendulum of death will swing back and forth for ever.

Killing is not victory in Shakespeare, and except in a relative sense it is not even death: its grim result is a revenge-seeking ghost. The dead men in his plays are in some respects more powerful than the living; and retaliation from beyond the grave is not confined to cases of villainous murder, although it is more conspicuous in them. Many people would approve the deed of Brutus—he was not an evil man; but Caesar's ghost had power to destroy him. No one blames Romeo for killing Tybalt, and yet Juliet says:

> O, look! methinks I see my cousin's ghost
> Seeking out Romeo, that did spit his body
> Upon a rapier's point. Stay, Tybalt, stay!
>
> IV. iv

But Tybalt gets his man. It is the law with Shakespeare that the measure his characters mete is meted to them again: death does not close the account, from generation to generation it continues to be rendered, mounting to a general doom. The final outcome would be the self-destruction of mankind; and this can be prevented only—in Shakespeare's scheme—by those who have the wisdom, the love and the courage to forgive.

But Shakespearean forgiveness is not a passive quality; it is a regenerating power, and at its highest it is the prerogative of the perfect man. It is to gain self-perfection, therefore, that all his rising characters must have experience of the life removed. And that is why Orlando and the senior duke do not have recourse to arms, but withdraw into the forest to conquer the usurping powers in themselves, to win self-sovereignty and discover love, and to emerge from it with the strength to make a perfect conquest of their enemies. The forest is the place where truth, which is one with divine beauty, is found.

When we are prepared for this, by many parallels, the first speech of the duke in the forest—the opening of the second act—gives us the key phrases that unlock the parable. This speech has had the misfortune to become a standard recitation; and we must therefore try to disperse the fog of familiarity by which it is obscured, and receive a new impression.

It is often said that in *As You Like It* Shakespeare's aim is to show the superiority of the rustic over the courtly life. This ingenuous misconception is one outcome of the pernicious tendency to sentimentalize Shakespearean comedy, which has done so much to keep its true nature concealed. Shakespeare is not a whit less serious in comedy than in tragedy: to maintain otherwise is to argue that heaven is less significant than hell. The way to heaven may be less familiar; it is a destination for which few dramatists set out; and for that very reason it is the more important to realize that Shakespeare's thoughts do reach there.

No one supposes that the path is easy. The forest symbolizes one stage of the upward journey: it is adversity, although its uses are sweet; it is an exile from human society, necessary that the soul may know and harmonize itself; it is a place where the characters are brought to the brink of death, that the power of the spirit may be proved. And it is a place they leave,

returning to full participation in the life of men, when
the great discovery has been made. The forest has its
beauties and its compensations; it is better than the
"*envious* court"; but the court that the duke will
eventually set up—like that of the returning Prospero
—will be the court of a philosopher king. And to
maintain that Shakespeare sees the rustic life as
superior to that, is a falsification.

Throughout his career Shakespeare put this allegory
into his plays. It is the "naked hermitage" in which the
King of Navarre is tested by "frosts and fasts, hard
lodging and thin weeds". It is the forest of the outlaws,
in which Valentine is offered the choice of rulership or
death. And then—to leap across the years to *The
Tempest*—it is the voyage and the island, of which
Gonzalo says:

> O, rejoice
> Beyond a common joy! and set it down
> With gold on lasting pillars: In one voyage
> Did Claribel her husband find at Tunis,
> And Ferdinand, her brother, found a wife
> Where he himself was lost, *Prospero his dukedom*
> *In a poor isle, and all of us ourselves*
> *When no man was his own.*   T. V. i

Is it possible for anyone to be more consistent than
that—throughout the full span of his work? All these
characters, during a sojourn in the wilderness, *find
themselves*. And this is no mere figure of speech, but
the crowning event of a divine plan, for Gonzalo has
just said:

> Look down, you gods. . . .
> For it is you that have chalk'd forth the way
> Which brought us hither.

And yet nearly all Shakespeare's commentators dismiss his allegory, unstudied, with a curt negation. This prejudice, it seems to me, stands like a barricade across the path of criticism—and it must be stormed.

As You Like It is a central play, and reading the duke's first speech in the light of our knowledge of what has been and what will be, we find at once the familiar landmarks. "The seasons' difference", "the icy fang" of the wind—such bitter experience has, in the duke's estimation, one great value:

> —these are counsellers
> That feelingly persuade me what I am.   II. i

The theme of self-discovery is always revived by Shakespeare in precisely the context where allegory demands it. And it is achieved by finding something— not the "many a thousand grains that issue out of dust" and which are "not thyself"—something that the rough elements cannot touch: a spiritual self, whose love has the power to bring harmony on earth, and whose beauty is a revelation of heaven. It is a discovery of splendour without limit, and the soul that knows itself—

> Finds tongues in trees, books in the running brooks,
> Sermons in stones, and good in everything.

The remainder of this scene is devoted to the forest deer, and in particular to

> —a poor sequestered stag,
> That from the hunter's aim had ta'en a hurt.   II. i

Shakespeare frequently passes in this way from general statement to particular illustration—from the perception of the unifying good in all, to the consequent sense of compassion and kinship with one sentient creature.

His sympathies, as is well known, are always with the hunted[1]; but it is also worth remarking on the care with which his feelings are submitted to his reason.

As always, constancy to love is the quality that is tested most; and allegory accordingly requires that the two characters—Celia and Adam—who went into exile for love alone should be selected for this demonstration. "Do not seek", Celia had said to Rosalind, "to bear your griefs yourself and leave me out." And Adam had elected to follow his young master "to the last gasp with truth and loyalty". Both chose to make this sacrifice; and it is further evidence that the forest is a place of testing—not of idyllic escapism—that both are brought almost to death. We hear the same first words from each of them in the forest: "I can go no further." And Adam continues: "Here lie I down, and measure out my grave."

In this extremity, help comes—to the girls from the shepherd, to Orlando and Adam from the duke.

*   *   *

The third act in Shakespeare is always the one in which the dark forces, those tending to a tragic outcome, are most exerted. In tragedies, therefore, a decisive action, usually a killing, takes place: Tybalt, Caesar, Polonius, for example, are all killed by the hero in the third act, and the deed is a turning-point in each play. In comedies, the third act is merely one of error and confusion; and the decisive event takes place in the fourth act, which belongs to the powers of light. Since we are moving to a life-ending in *As You Like It*,

1 See C. Spurgeon, *Shakespeare's Imagery*, chapter VI.

the third act is inconclusive, a phase of mistakes rather than crimes.

It opens, characteristically, with a threat. Oliver is brought before the usurper Frederick and ordered, on pain of his own banishment and the confiscation of his lands, to find Orlando and bring him to court "dead or living". The plot fails, of course; and both the bad characters are finally converted.

Touchstone tries to trick Audrey into a faked marriage in this act, remarking aside: "—not being well married, it will be a good excuse for me hereafter to leave my wife". Jaques prevents this, and the couple are truly wedded at the end of the play. Phebe, here, scorns Silvius, and falls in love with Rosalind thinking her to be a young man. This knot of error is also untied later, partly by Rosalind and partly by the constancy of Silvius. But the most important thing in this act is, of course, the constancy of Orlando—first in a real separation, then in a seeming one, when he woos Rosalind in disguise. Again we find the familiar sequence: the tests of love, the disguise, the piercing of it, and at last the union with true beauty. And we have the usual signs, pointing to the divine nature of the ultimate revelation, to the need for self-knowledge and a gradual ascent. When Orlando determines to hang tongues on every tree, he continues:

> But upon the fairest boughs,
>   Or at every sentence' end,
> Will I Rosalinda write;
>   Teaching all that read, to know
> The quintessence of every sprite
>   Heaven would in little show.   III. ii

With the Platonist background in mind, we see at once that this is not a fanciful but a theoretical poem. And to emphasize the fact, Shakespeare comes back to it a little later, pointing to the inner nature of all Orlando's odes and elegies again:

—all, forsooth, deifying the name of Rosalind.

III. ii

"Deifying" links them with what we have already noticed about "heavenly Rosalind", and of her predecessors in other plays: it is not the girl, but what she stands for that is being described by such words, definition and not hyperbole is intended. But even when we have recognized this, we may still underestimate the degree to which Shakespeare is drawing on an established philosophical system at this point. After particularizing Rosalind's beauties, Orlando goes on:

Thus Rosalind of many parts
By heavenly synod was devised,
Of many faces, eyes, and hearts
To have the touches dearest prized.

This is evidently based on a meditative phase—quite appropriate to Orlando's present solitude—of the "inner ascent" to Beauty. In Castiglione's scheme, from which Shakespeare probably derived it, it is stage three:

The lover . . . shall gather in his thought by litle and litle so many ornaments, that meddling all beautie together, he shal make an universall conceite, and bring the multitude of them to the unitie of one alone, that is generally spred over the nature of man. And thus shall he beholde no more the particular beautie of one woman, but an universall, that decketh out all bodies.

That was "Platonism" of the period, and there would have been nothing recondite about it to a sixteenth-century poet: it would have been as familiar to Shakespeare as, we might say, the theories of Freud and Jung are to a modern playwright. Benivieni, who did much to diffuse, and in some measure to shape, Renaissance Neo-Platonism, says substantially the same. The soul must mount, step by step, to the uncreated origin:

> —quinc' elevando
> Di grado in grado se nell' increato
> Sol torna—

And at a particular degree of the ascent it must assemble in imagination many beauties and combine them into one concept of quintessential beauty:

> —indi di varie et molte
> Belta, dal corpo sciolte,
> Form un concetto, in cui quel che natura
> Divis'ha in tutti, in un pinge e figura.[1]

Fletcher's admirable comment on this stanza makes it plain how great an amount of analytical thinking lay behind all poetry of this kind:

It is the "sweet error" of love that it thus in imagination sees the loved object fairer than it is——at least to others. Still, perfect beauty is not "full expressed" in the sensuous image, not even perfect sensuous beauty. The image, however glorified, is of a particular "fairness", which only participates in but does not fully express, its perfect type: so as the Greek painter is said to have shaped his perfect type of beautiful woman by combining in one the

[1] *Canzona dello Amore Celeste et Divino*, stanza vii.

beauties of a hundred women, the Soul now—Grade III—"from many fairs torn from matter", i.e. from many subjective images of particular fairness, forms the image, still sensuous indeed, of the type. . . . In Grade III, the Soul rejoices in the universalized conception of sensible Beauty, still believing the principle of Beauty therein contained to be given her by the Sensible World. But reflecting on this principle, the Soul discovers that the Sensible World has given but the raw material, and that the principle itself of Beauty is of her own making, and is only the reflection of the divine Ideas as conceived by her. . . .[1]

The lover must, therefore, pass on to the fourth stage, looking within himself—opening "the eyes that all men have, and few occupie"—to which we have already alluded.

One special value of Orlando's verses is the insight they afford to us of Shakespeare's mind at work: and its activity is seen to be remote from that of thoughtless genius pouring out an unpremeditated song. He could do that too, of course; but he was also a highly "intentionalist" poet, writing to an ascertainable plan. In this case, he is carefully constructing one recognized step in the "Platonic" ascent, the combining of particular beauties—

> Helen's cheek, but not her heart,
>   Cleopatra's majesty,
> Atalanta's better part,
>   Sad Lucretia's modesty

[1] J. B. Fletcher, "Benivieni's Ode of Love and Spenser's Fowre Hymnes', in *Modern Philology*, vol. viii, 1911, University of Chicago.

into a universal—
> The quintessence of every sprite.

And this, again in accordance with Marsilian theory, is part of a movement towards self-knowledge, that is, knowledge of the veiled divinity in man. That is a theme Shakespeare never omits; and in this act the advice is given to a character who badly needs it, when Rosalind says to Phebe:

> But, mistress, know yourself: down on your knees,
> And thank Heaven, fasting, for a good man's love—

Phebe is being particularly invited to know her faults. This is the negative and not unnecessary aspect of self-discovery; but it is the positive side, as is made clear in the next act, with which Shakespeare is chiefly concerned.

*　　*　　*

As in every play that is moving to a life-ending, the decisive action takes place in the fourth act. Habitually, in the regeneration dramas, the villain is placed at the mercy of the hero he has wronged: this is a supreme temptation to the hero to betray the principle of love —which he has the power and, by conventional standards of justice, the right to do—and to exact retribution, "death for death", or whatever the debt may be. If he does this, he can hardly be called culpable. It is consistent with human law; it satisfies the audience; it is the conclusion, for example, of *Macbeth*. But it is not Shakespeare's idea of a perfect ending; for it is not the action taken by any one of his heroes who has learnt, in the wilderness, to be constant to love and true to himself.

There is something more than the obvious contrast

in tone between the ending of most of the tragedies (I exclude *Hamlet*) and the regeneration plays: it is the difference between a return to stable government in the conventional sense and the achievement of an ideal rulership: the one is more or less realistic, the other, if you will, visionary. Scotland under Malcolm, the Roman Empire under Octavius, are subjects for an historian; but the kind of government we must envisage as about to be established at the close of *As You Like It*, *Measure for Measure* or *The Tempest* are subjects not, I maintain, for the dreaming escapist, but for the philosopher. There is a similarity about them, an idea compounded probably from many sources—the philosopher kings of Plato, the ideal of perfect Christian kingship, the Virgilian prophesy *redeunt Saturnia regna*—and these are fused in Shakespeare's mind, not into a reverie, but into an aspiration of what kingship ought to be. Not one of these "perfect" rulers comes to his own by violence; but each, through his sojourn in the wilderness, acquires a spiritual quality—a kind of *mana* or *tao*—that is irresistible power because it is in perfect alignment with the will of heaven. These are the kings of a returning age of gold, to whose dominions the maiden of true Justice will come back:

> This, this, and only such as this,
> The bright Astraea's region is,
>   Where she would pray to live,
> And in the midst of so much gold,
> Unbought with grace, or fear unsold,
>   The law to mortals give.[1]

[1] Ben Jonson, *The Golden Age Restored*, 1616.

The restoration of a golden age was a great deal more in Shakespeare's mind than it was in Jonson's. It is not merely a pleasant fantasy with him, because it is deduced from a principle to which he firmly holds: when perfect self-sovereignty has been achieved in the soul, it will become a transforming power in the world, and there will be no need for recourse to arms. During the life removed, the soul discovers that through being receptive to the spirit it becomes mysteriously creative of harmony on earth; and so the hero who has undergone this experience emerges as not only a man of vision but also of divine power. The dethroned duke exemplifies this in *As You Like It*. But dramatically he is a background figure, and the active ethic of spiritual achievement is shown to us in Orlando.

Oliver, it will be remembered, has been ordered by the usurping duke to find his brother dead or alive, and he comes to the forest to do so. He almost loses his own life in the attempt; and Orlando discovers him asleep under a tree—lost, starving and in rags, a snake coiled round his neck, while a lioness

> Lay crouching, head on ground, with catlike
> watch,
> When that the sleeping man should stir—— IV. iii

Orlando is tempted. The enemy who plotted his destruction is now at his mercy. The principles of love and justice are in the balance. If he walks away, Oliver must meet the death he has deserved.

> Twice did he turn his back and purposed so;
> But kindness, nobler ever than revenge,
> And nature, stronger than his just occasion,
> Made him give battle to the lioness—— IV. iii

He kills the lioness, and is himself wounded; but there is much more to the situation than this surface. The fact that he has been constant to love and to "nature"— that is, to his own true nature—confers on him, according to Shakespeare's regular scheme, the power to make creative mercy effective. The enmity is therefore destroyed. And just as Valentine was able to give "Silvia" to Proteus—that is, to bestow on him as a gift the vision of true beauty that he himself had won by merit—so now Orlando's perfect forgiveness awakens Oliver to the knowledge of his real self. He recounts this in a conversation with the heroines.

> CELIA: Are you his brother?
> ROSALIND: Was it you he rescued?
> CELIA: Was't you that did so oft contrive to kill
> him?
> OLIVER: 'Twas I; but 'tis not I. I do not shame
> To tell you what I was, since my conversion
> So sweetly tastes, being the thing I am.
> IV. iii

In drama after drama, Shakespeare comes back to the supreme experience of self-discovery. The regenerating hero achieves it by merit; and he bestows it on his former enemy by grace. We find this conception in *The Two Gentlemen of Verona*—one of the earliest comedies; we have it here, in a central play; and it occurs in what is possibly the last. With Prospero's help, Gonzalo tells us in *The Tempest*, the characters all found themselves, "When no man was his own." However reluctant many people may be to admit allegory in Shakespeare, I think everyone will agree

that this life-long consistency demands some explanation.

It is indisputable that we have a long line of heroes
who spend a period withdrawn from the world—in
hermitage, forest, or desert isle—and who return to
society spiritually awakened and able to awaken
others. Shakespeare alters his source-stories deliberately
in order that this pattern may recur. The only reasonable explanation, I submit, is that of parable or
allegory. And it is significant that the allegorical
interpretation comes to the commentator's rescue
precisely in those episodes where psychological analysis
lets him down. We have noticed this, for instance, in
the conclusion of *The Two Gentlemen of Verona*, which
has left many critics baffled and annoyed. There are
three outstanding instances of similar character in
As You Like It. All of them, by general consent, are
inadequately motivated from the psychological point
of view, and therefore seem weak: all, when considered
as allegory, are found to be not merely strong, but
indispensable. One of these is the instantaneous
conversion of Oliver; but there are much greater
surprises in the fifth act.

*   *   *

The opening surprise in the fifth act is the love-
match between Oliver and Celia. This is usually
dismissed as a marriage of dramatic convenience. "The
loyal Celia," it has been remarked, "has to be rewarded
in some way". True; but it still seems odd, by normal
standards of psychology and construction, that to wed
the "villain" should be her recompense. She has no

sooner set eyes on the reformed Oliver, however, than she falls in love with him; and a marriage is promptly arranged—a piece of feeble characterization, it is sometimes thought, which may be pardoned because it is necessary to round out the happy ending: in other words, Shakespeare has united the one-time villain with the character whose outstanding quality is self-sacrificing love, and his only reason for doing so is to get a good curtain. Is it really necessary to be resigned to this lame and rather cynical conclusion?

The career of Oliver conforms to a pattern that is peculiarly Shakespearean; and this is designed, I think, not primarily for a dramatic purpose—it has a notable weakness from that point of view—but because it illustrates an ethic in which Shakespeare believed. One instance of many in support of this proposition is the resemblance between Oliver and Proteus.

Proteus was a knave, he did not quite qualify as a villain, who was eventually redeemed by two things —the perfect forgiveness of Valentine and the self-sacrificing love of Julia. This event, an abrupt conversion took place in a forest; and Valentine's magnanimity, which was indispensable to the miracle, was itself the crowning act of a period of forest-exile, wherein his constancy to love had been tested and found true.

How close this is in design and feeling to the predicament of Oliver. For him also it is through the creative mercy of a brother-enemy—who has, like Valentine, won self-sovereignty in the wilderness—that his own realization of his higher nature comes. Up

118

to this point, however, the plot has not provided him with a sweetheart; but the character who has been built up—not in the source-story, but deliberately by Shakespeare—into the type of unselfish love is now united with him. When we further remember that self-sovereignty, love and the revelation of true beauty are invariably related in Shakespeare, we begin to see a philosophic pattern predominantly Christian Platonist: the construction then ceases to be merely a matter of romantic expediency, and takes on coherence and strength.

Shakespeare, of course, set no value whatsoever on originality of plot—he took his stories from anyone and anywhere: all depends on the way they are retold. And his first step in doing this must have been to re-shape the source-story according to a definite scheme. The five-act structure of Terence is its backbone; it is this construction that allots the third act particularly to the "dark" forces, and the fourth act to those of "light".[1]

But integrated with this dramatic pattern there is also an ethical or philosophic one. The hero is always shown to be moving either towards or away from self-realization and love—to cosmos or to chaos. And for Shakespeare this means the difference between a comedy or life-play and a tragedy or death-play. It is essential to understand that his comedies are no less profound in intention than his tragedies.

Oliver was moving towards a death-ending until he discovered himself—"the thing I am". This, in Shakespeare's undermeaning, is a spiritual awakening,

[1] I have discussed this in *Shakespeare and the Rose of Love*.

and union with divine love and beauty is a part of the experience; therefore, on the hypothesis that the play is an allegory of the ascent as conceived by Marsilian Platonism, his marriage to Celia is indispensable.

It should hardly be necessary to add that the presentation of this allegory, which would not have seemed abstruse to the educated members of his audience, is only one part of Shakespeare's intention: no one, I imagine, doubts that he aimed to please a general public as well. Those who perceive the allegory gain an additional delight: nothing of the familiar beauty is lost to them, but a new dimension is uncovered. Those who deny it are confined to surfaces:

> Some there be that shadows kiss,
> Such have but a shadow's bliss.

Shakespeare says many times and in many ways that "the great globe itself" and everything upon it is an "insubstantial pageant" and its pleasures brief. If, then, he aimed to please truly—to give more than a shadow's bliss—his own argument would have led him to present an inner world. The pageant, he tells us, will fade and "leave not a rack behind"; but the actors are "all spirits", and physical dissolution, we must suppose, will leave their reality untouched. Since Shakespeare had this conviction, his allegory is of necessity concerned with self-discovery in the spiritual sense. When his characters achieve this, they have union with imperishable beauty, and give birth in consequence to virtue and power; when they do not, every one of them is shown to be like Proteus, worshipping a mere portrait of beauty:

To that I'll speak, to that I'll sign and weep;
For since the substance of your perfect self
Is else devoted, I am but a shadow,
And to your shadow will I make true love.

T.G.V. IV. ii

That is what Shakespeare means by "a shadow's bliss".
And it is quite another thing from the true delight to
which his ascending characters are led. It is this—
"measure heap'd in joy"—that will be the reward of
Orlando. He has passed all his tests—and so, I think
we are to understand, has the exiled duke; if, therefore,
the allegory is to be continued to its ideal climax, what
must now be shown, so far as it is possible in the
theatre, is the revelation of the "inmost faire". Orlando
and the duke have both deserved this, but to present
it on the stage is a tremendous challenge to playwright
and producer. That Rosalind should take off her
disguise and appear as her natural self is necessary, but
not enough: that would satisfy the romance, but it
would be inadequate for the parable.

In the first act, we recall, she was "heavenly
Rosalind". Later we were told that she "by heavenly
synod was devised", and her name was "deified". Now,
the showing forth of this divinity is what Shakespeare
must attempt. We expect her to return to the assembled
characters as a woman, that will not provide us with
an awakening surprise; and therefore, so that our eyes
may be opened to her heavenly nature, she is led back
on the stage by a god.

Hymen from heaven brought her.   V. iv

This is the ideal climax, both dramatically and allegorically: the curtains of mortality are parted, and we see

121

beings who taste a spirit's bliss—a glimpse of startling glory; but upon reflection, we find that pure logic has brought us to this close, and that the Platonic parable could have culminated in nothing else than an epiphany of the celestial Venus.

If Shakespeare ever produced his own plays, it would be particularly interesting to know how he contrived this theophany. Hymen, we may suppose, would have worn a robe of saffron, been crowned with flowers, and borne a lighted torch; his attendants would have been heavenly beings; but Rosalind, in her supreme moment, must have outshone them all. It is worth noticing that immediately before the entrance of the god and his retinue, bringing her "from heaven", we have Touchstone's great scene, with his two celebrated speeches on the lie. This arrangement strongly suggests the construction—brought to great excellence a few years later by Ben Jonson—of antimasque and masque. The purpose of the antimasque was to enhance, by contrast, the brilliant disclosure of the masque itself, which was intended to astound the audience with a sudden breathtaking splendour. Before this scene came the antimasque, usually comic, but occasionally horrific.[1] Those who designed such spectacles for the court of James I may well have owed some ideas to Shakespeare; and conversely, our knowledge of the court masque may give us a hint of the kind of effect at which Shakespeare aimed. The purpose of his present contrast—a speech on falsehood and a vision of truth —is also to awaken by splendour. And since the

[1] As in Jonson's, *The Masque of Queens*, 1609.

masque was always allegorical, there is yet more
reason to think that in his comparable scenes Shakespeare approved the dictum of Ben Jonson:

> . . . though their voice be taught to sound to present
> occasions, their sense or doth or should always lay
> hold on more removed mysteries.[1]

Even without this corroboration, we should be irresist-
ibly drawn to the conclusion that some more removed
mystery was in Shakespeare's mind, for the whole of
this play has prepared us for a revelation.

Looking back, we now see that five phases of the
"Platonic" ascent, as Castiglione and other Renaissance
writers schematized it, have been enacted between
Orlando and Rosalind. As this is of great importance
to an understanding of Shakespeare's intentions, I
hope some slight repetition will be excused if I
recapitulate the five.

1 According to the accepted pattern, the lover's
first step is to be enchanted by the bodily beauty
of a particular woman.

This happens to Orlando—in Act I, scene ii—
when he first sets eyes on Rosalind.

2 In the absence of his lady, the solitary lover
re-creates her beauty to his imagination, and
"shall evermore carrie his precious treasure
about with him shutte fast within his hart".

We may assume that Orlando has re-created
her in his heart as well as engraved her on the
trees when—in Act III, scene ii—he says:

> Run, run, Orlando; carve on every tree
> The fair, the chaste and unexpressive she.

[1] *Hymenaei*, preface, 1606.

3 The lover gathers in his thoughts many particular beauties, and "he shal make an universal conceit and bring the multitude of them to the unitie of one alone".

In the same scene, as we have already noticed at length, Orlando conceives a "universal" Rosalind:

Of many faces, eyes and hearts,
To have the touches dearest prized.

4 The lover is advised that "in steade of going out of his wit with thought . . . he may come into his wit, to behold the beautie that is seen with the eyes of the minde. . . ."

In Act V, scene ii, Orlando exclaims: "I can live no more by thinking". To which the disguised Rosalind promptly replies that by an act of magic —"most profound . . . and yet not damnable"— she will set the real Rosalind before him on the morrow. And this must surely mean that Orlando has had the heavenly beauty with him all the time, but that until "the eyes of the minde" have been thus magically opened, he cannot recognize it.

5 The lover's soul "no more shadowed with the darke night of earthly matters, seeth the heavenly beautie".

In the last scene, Rosalind is brought "from heaven", and presented to Orlando by a god.

That the sixth and seventh stages should be left to our imagination is reasonable, if not inevitable. But the first five have been enacted; and in view of the considerable technicality involved, I think most people will agree that this could not have happened by chance. If the ascent is at the heart of the plan here, then it becomes more likely that our detection of it in the earlier plays was correct; and if we conclude that Shakespeare made regular use of it, a fascinating vista begins to open. I think we shall find that the principle of the heroine's symbolic nature is a constant element; and that Ophelia, Desdemona, Hermione and Cordelia stand for the Heavenly Beauty rejected, with tragic consequences, just as definitely and deliberately as Rosalind stands for its acceptance.

When we first considered Castiglione's stages, it will be remembered, we noticed that from the theatrical point of view the loss of the heroine created a problem. I think it may now be granted that Shakespeare came to grips with this problem and solved it brilliantly: by the device of putting the heroine in disguise, she was preserved for the audience, but seemingly lost to the hero for that part of the ascent which had to be made in solitude, and restored to him as a revelation, undisguised, on its completion.

With the appearance of the "heavenly Rosalind", all knots of error are simultaneously untied; and we are particularly invited, as at the close of other plays, to reflect how these "most strange events" have come about:

> Feed yourselves with questioning;
> That reason wonder may diminish,
> How thus we met, and these things finish. V. iv

In both tragedy and comedy, Shakespeare clearly wishes his audience not merely to admire but also to comprehend his closing demonstration. If it is death, then—

> See what a scourge is laid upon your hate!

If it is a renewal of life—

> How comes this gentle concord in the world?

Always the tableau and its haunting question. Why does the curtain fall upon that sorrow or this joy? We are not only urged to lay hold on these "mysteries", we are promised their interpretation:

> Put not yourselves into amazement how these things should be: all difficulties are but easy when they are known.

And since what is being required of us is to diminish wonder by the use of reason, how ought we to explain the final incident of this play—the reinstatement of the rightful duke? In the source-story the usurper Frederick was defeated in battle, but in Shakespeare's version he—

> Address'd a mighty power; which were on foot,
> In his own conduct, purposely to take
> His brother here and put him to the sword:
> And to the skirts of this wild wood he came;
> Where meeting with an old religious man,
> After some question with him, was converted
> Both from his enterprise and from the world,
> His crown bequeathing to his banish'd brother,
> And all their lands restored to them again
> That were with him exiled.   V. iv

Why did Shakespeare make this change? Was it because *As You Like It* is a pleasant play, and he did not want to admit anything into it that could distress? That is doubtless a part of the explanation; but if it were the whole, it leaves us with a trivial story. The allegory, however, that I have endeavoured to trace requires precisely such a climax; and it therefore seems to me reasonable—indeed, imperative—to give full weight to it, and to recognize the conclusion as a victory of the spirit. If we do, there is no weakness in the plot that stands in need of excuse; the original story has been re-shaped by a lucid and logical intelligence.

Many critics, of course, maintain that Shakespeare had no second purpose in any of his plays, and that it is inadmissible to speak of them as parables. Having held this opinion myself, it is one that I appreciate; but the evidence has forced me to disavow it, and I think there is a flaw in the argument on which it rests. To picture Shakespeare simply as a man of the theatre, whose one aim was to please his public and satisfy a purely professional or aesthetic sense of dramatic craftsmanship in himself, may appear to be most reasonable; but in point of fact it is to impute to him a modern mentality that it would have been next to impossible for him to have had. He could not have conceived the scope of important human actions to be confined to this world alone; the doctrine of "correspondences" was still too potent in the imagination of his age. An interpretation, then, that would be common sense if applied to the drama of our century, becomes far-fetched if carried back to his; and conversely, a comedy which is also a Platonic parable—a composition most improbable to-day—would have come naturally to Shakespeare. The philosophic ideas that underlie his romantic plots would have reached him, even if he had not used them, from many contemporary sources: they are the ripples of thought that spread through the mind of Europe from the Platonic Academy in

Florence. One such idea seems particularly worth noticing in our present context:

> "Be careful," Ficino wrote to the young Lorenzo de'Medici, "never to despise humanity, nor to look on it as merely earth-born and mortal; for humanity is a being of beauty, of celestial origin, and the greatest joy of God in heaven."[1]

The assertion leads to an ideal of government which was sincerely held and the outcome of consistent thinking: it may not be practical, but it is not merely fanciful. And in commenting on this letter, Saitta observes:

> This principle is a forceful rejection of irrational authority and despotism. Only by humanity can humanity be ruled: only the spirit will dominate the spirit. Any other domination is extrinsic, contrary to nature, and impotent. We have here a vivid portrait of Renaissance man—aspiring with all his strength to found a true humanity, one that will reveal all the powers of its origin, and be moulded by the beauty of the spirit. . . . Ficino's fervent admiration of the beauty of mankind arises from his deep intuition of the place in the universe that awaits us. For had he not affirmed that the ray of divine light, which penetrates everywhere, exists in the stone but does not live there, lives in the plant but does not shine there, shines in the animal but is not there reflected to its fount, while in man it exists, lives, shines, and reflects its origin?

> *L'umanità non si domina che con l'umanità: solo lo spirito puo dominare lo spirito. Qualunque altro dominio è estrinseco, innaturale, impotente.*[2]

[1] *Letters*, Book V, p. 805.
[2] Giuseppe Saitta, *La Filosofia di Marsilio Ficino*, Casa Editrice G. Principato, 1923, p. 172.

When we see that conceptions of perfect government, quite comparable with Shakespeare's seeming flights of fancy, were a subject of correspondence between the most eminent philosopher and one of the most enlightened rulers of the fifteenth century, we are no longer entitled to dismiss the Shakespearean counterpart as a mere theatrical device. The Christian humanism of the Renaissance had a vision of government entirely different from anything we now associate with politics; and I suggest that this prophetic faith is being affirmed by implication in *As You Like It*, *Measure for Measure* and *The Tempest*. It is not unless we appreciate this, that we shall see the inner splendour of Shakespearean thought.

The rule of Oliver and the usurping duke typify the kind of government that the human spirit cannot, by its very nature, accept. And that is why Orlando says in the first scene:

> This it is, Adam, that grieves me; and the spirit of my father, which I think is within me, begins to mutiny against this servitude.

With the help of Marsilianism, the meaning of the parable becomes clear. In Orlando, the divine spirit is waking to self-consciousness; and when this happens, it will not and cannot be dominated by brute strength. Nor, if it is to remain true to itself, can it overcome brutality with brutality. Therefore, Orlando continues:

> I will no longer endure it, though yet
> I know no wise remedy how to avoid it.

He finds the remedy with Rosalind in the forest, as Valentine found it in the forest with Silvia. In Platonic terms, it is the union of the soul with perfect beauty, whence perfect virtue springs. In the language of Christian humanism, it is the awakening of the divine in man, through acceptance of the sovereignty of love. There is no real difference: and the result is the power to make the perfect conquest with which the play concludes. What we uncover then, among so many other things, is a parable of government—the only kind of government that will be finally acceptable to enlightened man: *solo lo spirito puo dominare lo spirito*.

Chapter VII

"ALL'S WELL THAT ENDS WELL"

ALL'S WELL THAT ENDS WELL is one of the problem plays. The style of some passages is early, and that of others mature. It has been suggested that it is a recast of *Love's Labour's Wonne*—the vanished companion of *Love's Labour's Lost*, referred to by Meres in 1598. This is only a speculation; but it would account for the incongruities of style and content—an affinity, on the one hand, with the early comedies, and on the other with the central plays, *Troilus and Cressida*, *Hamlet* and *Measure for Measure*. The date of 1602, for the final version, was once widely accepted; and although it has been challenged, it still seems to me the most reasonable guess. In the main, it is supported by the play's philosophical ideas: there are strong traces of medievalism in the heroine, but more developed Renaissance conceptions are to be found in her as well. And it is principally these that I should like to explore.

In the opening, the young Count Bertram de Rousillon is about to leave his home, for the first time, to complete his social education at the court of the King of France. He also leaves behind him an adoring girl, Helena, who has never declared her love, and of whose devotion he is unaware. We might perhaps expect that he, or they, will be subjected to the now-familiar series of Shakespearean tests; and this is, in fact, what happens. Bertram fails decisively, but he is finally redeemed by Helena's unfailing love. The pattern is clearly reminiscent of *The Two Gentlemen of Verona*—the saving of Proteus largely by the self-giving of Julia. This is the leading theme of the play, and the principle it rests on comes, of course, straight from the Gospels.

The chief characteristic of Renaissance philosophy is the blending of Christianity with Neo-Platonism. And if we ask ourselves, "Is there any sign of Neo-Platonism —or, more precisely, of Marsilianism—in this first scene?" we find that there is. At first sight, this discovery may not seem of much importance; but I hope to show that it provides us with a clue, most helpful in the solution of the major problems of this perplexing play.

Bertram has a mother, but his father is dead, and Helena is an orphan; but while his father was a count, hers was only a physician, albeit a celebrated one— Gerard of Narbon—and so in rank she is greatly beneath him. That is why she has never disclosed her love, and he never suspected it. But she imparts her secret feelings to us, directly after his casual leave-taking, in her first soliloquy:

> —my imagination
> Carries no favour in't but Bertram's.
> I am undone: there is no living, none,
> If Bertram be away. 'Twere all one
> That I should love a bright particular star
> And think to wed it, he is so above me:
> In his bright radiance and collateral light
> Must I be comforted, not in his sphere.   I. i

Now, even the bitter-sweet of daily seeing him is over, and only her mind-drawn portrait remains. But the soliloquy tells us more than the fact of Helena's heart-break: it also suggests that Shakespeare wrote it with Castiglione's stages of the ascent in his mind. It moves from bodily presence—

> 'Twas pretty, though a plague,
> To see him every hour—

through an imaginative re-creation of the physical form—

> —to sit and draw
> His arched brows, his hawking eye, his curls,
> In our heart's table—

towards spiritualization—

> But now he's gone, and my idolatrous fancy
> Must sanctify his reliques.   I. i

I feel that Shakespeare would not have phrased it in that way, unless he had been thinking of the ascent: the last line states precisely what the soul is supposed to do, in solitude and by its own effort, with material beauty. More theory is implicit in the whole speech than may at first appear; and the same is true of Helena's second soliloquy, with which the scene closes. In this, she faces her difficulties with a new resolve. Previously, she had accepted the insuperability of the barrier of rank but now she does not; resignation has changed to aspiration; and what her second speech really implies is that she has it in her power to make a spiritual ascent, and that if she does so, her rank will be made equal to his by her merit. The king amply confirms this standard of nobility later in the play; and at the close of it, Helena is above Bertram in every respect, being described by Lafeu as one—

> Whose dear perfection hearts that scorn'd to serve
> Humbly call'd mistress.   V. iii

Helena's gradual ascension points to issues of wider importance that we cannot dwell on here. But if we recall that in *As You Like It*, and elsewhere, one of Shakespeare's assertions was that the ultimate power is always spiritual, we shall appreciate that consistency requires the statement he is making here, namely, that spiritual rank has primacy of all other, and that in an ideal, or perhaps we should say in an unmasked society, social rank would be its reflection. The point Helena is aiming to establish is that everyone may achieve this ultimate nobility by an act of will. Indeed, if the inner ascent is made, nothing is impossible:

> Our remedies oft in ourselves do lie,
> Which we ascribe to heaven: the fated sky
> Gives us free scope—   I. i

In Shakespeare's view of fate, only "the duller parts" are under the power of the stars; always there is a quality in the soul whose freedom is intrinsic, but nothing will unlock this power, and confer divine liberty on man, except love. This is a general proposition in Shakespeare, but it is based on a more detailed theory to which he is in debt.

"Venus", says Ficino, quoting Orpheus, "commands fate." And he expounds this in Christian terms by saying, "The rule of Love is older than that of Necessity, since the power of Love begins in God, and the power of Necessity begins in created things."

Pico della Mirandola takes up this point in several passages, which make the background Platonism of the position quite clear: an embodied soul falls under the power of fate, because it has forgotten and so does not assert its divine nature; but the sight of beauty, in this world, awakens love; and although love is blind at first—that is, directed to shadows instead of substances—it is none the less an unconscious movement towards God, and brings an ever-increasing measure of power and freedom. Thomas Stanley translates one relevant passage from Pico rather quaintly:

> Those souls employ'd in corporeal office are depriv'd of contemplation, borrowing science from sense; to this wholly enclin'd; full of errours. Their onely means of release from this bondage is the amatory life; which by sensible beauties, exciting in the soul a remembrance of the intellectual, raiseth her from this terrene life to the eternal; by the flame of love refined into an Angel.[1]

It is only, I would suggest, when we give weight to this contemporary background that we can fully understand Shakespeare's continual play both on masks and the beauty behind the mask, and on the freedom and sovereignty conferred by love—which is, as it were, the common term between the soul and heaven. When Helena asks:

> What power is it which mounts my love so high;
> That makes me see, and cannot feed mine eye?
>
> I. i

many people in Shakespeare's audience would have

[1] *A Platonick Discourse upon Love*, edited E. G. Gardner, 1914, p. 17.

known that the power she felt, but could not yet recognize, was the will of God, which, in Marsilianism is identical with love. This explains why, so long as she is constant, she is able to exhibit powers that are partially divine—increasingly so as her tests are passed; and why, if she is faithful to the end, she must triumph.

It is not, therefore, essential to suppose from her next couplet—

The mightiest space in fortune nature brings
To join like likes and kiss like native things— I. i

that Shakespeare is also relying on the doctrine of companion souls to unite her with Bertram; but I think we should entertain this speculation as a probability. We have had hints in other plays that Spenser's version of the idea might have been in Shakespeare's mind; it would have been quite natural for him to have used it; and it fits into the present plot very neatly. There were many forms of the theory, besides Spenser's, on which Shakespeare could have drawn; and the phrase "kiss like *native* things" might point to the more astrological variety, of which Pico says:

Many imagine the Rational Soul descending from her Star, in her *Vehiculum Coeleste*, of her self forms the Body, to which by that Medium she is united. Our Author [Benivieni] upon these grounds supposeth, that into the *Vehiculum* of the Soul, by her endued with Power to form the body, is infused from her Star a particular formative vertue, distinct according to that Star . . . and that the figures of two Bodies being formed by the vertue of the same Star, this Conformity begets Love.[1]

[1] *Op. cit.*, p. 74.

That may be what Helena means; but as Shakespeare seldom or never follows a source exactly, taking only a seed of inspiration which he cultivates in his own way, it is vain to hope for more than a clue to his intention. On the whole, I think we might guess from this first scene, that Helena and Bertram are pre-destined for each other; that she is nearer to the recognition of this —piercing, that is to say, the disguise of the body by love-sight—than he is; and that it will be her constancy to the ideal of love that will bring about their mutual illumination. But at all events—by either way or by both ways—the barrier of rank can be surmounted; and we have the firm assurance, in her second soliloquy, that she will spare no pains in the attempt:

>   —who ever strove
> To show her merit, that did miss her love?   I. i

Bertram has gone to the court of the King of France, who suffers from a malady that none of his physicians is able to cure. Helena decides to follow him there, and, relying on some mysterious treatment, to attempt to recover the king. Her first intention is to show her merit. And it was Shakespeare's life-long asseveration that if our virtues do not "go forth of us", and in effect work miracles, we might as well not have them. The power that makes them go forth is love: and if Helena had not been in love with Bertram, she would never have thought of showing merit by healing the King of France. When the countess—Bertram's mother—insists on knowing the full reason for her journey to Paris, Helena admits as much, and hints at a great deal more:

My lord your son made me to think on this;
Else Paris, and the medecine, and the king,
Had from the conversation of my thoughts
Haply been absent then.
COUNTESS: But think you, Helen,
If you should tender your supposed aid,
He would receive it?
        . . . how shall they credit
A poor unlearned virgin, when the schools,
Embowell'd of their doctrine, have left off
The danger to itself?
HELENA: There's something in't,
More than my father's skill, which was the
    great'st
Of his profession, that this good receipt
Shall for my legacy be sanctified
By the luckiest stars in heaven . . .
COUNTESS: Dost thou believe 't?
HELENA: Ay, madam, knowingly.
COUNTESS: Why, Helen, thou shalt have my leave
and love. . . .
Be gone to-morrow; and be sure of this,
What I can help thee to, thou shalt not miss. I. iii

Twice in this act Helena has used the word sanctify;
and it becomes increasingly clear that love—besides
being physically consummated—is also to be raised,
according to the doctrine of the ascent, to the sphere
of the spirit. If we try to explain Helena by character-
analysis alone, we may as well give up hope of fathom-
ing the play: she has significance as a figure in a
parable, in addition to her personality, and both her
aspects must be taken account of.

We have been prepared, by this dialogue, for the
customary Shakespearean miracle: I say customary,
because although it is seldom as obvious as here, the

miraculous is always associated with the rising soul in Shakespeare. This ought not to surprise us; for it is logically inseparable from the idea of the gradual emancipation of the love-guided soul from fate; and Shakespeare never falters on this principle. It is not, of course, exclusively his; and like so many kindred thoughts that were widely disseminated in the Renaissance, we can trace it to its fountain-head in Ficino:

—love is free, and rises of its own accord in free will, which not even God, who decreed that it should be free in the very beginning, controls. Hence it happens that love, which rules over all, escapes the power of all.[1]

In Shakespeare, however, this sovereignty is not easily asserted; the baser elements rebel; and in his plays, love must be prepared to endure all, before it rules all.

* * *

As we have been told, the most learned doctors have done their utmost in treating the King of France; and they have all come to the conclusion that his complaint is irremediable. He himself is of the same opinion, and so firmly set in it that he would rather die on the advice of his physicians than attempt an unorthodox cure. He receives Helena kindly; but in spite of her father's reputation, he looks on her as a well-intentioned quack. He is grateful; but the President of the British Medical Association himself could not have rejected her aid more firmly:

[1] See Appendix II.

139

> I say we must not
> So stain our judgement, or corrupt our hope,
> To prostitute our past-cure malady
> To emperics, or to dissever so
> Our great self and our credit, to esteem
> A senseless help—   II. i

Very tactfully, however, while seeming to accept this decision, Helena continues to plead. And she presents her case in words that shed a further light on the divine significance of the heroine in Shakespeare. Many critics may still maintain—although in the face of the accumulated evidence I do not think it is a sound opinion—that when the hero sees "heaven" in the heroine that is merely a figure of speech. But no one will deny that Helena exhibits divine qualities in relation to the king. She is being presented indubitably as an agent of grace when she says:

> He that of greatest works is finisher,
> Oft does them by the weakest minister:
> So holy writ in babes hath judgement shown,
> When judges have been babes. . . .
> Oft expectation fails, and most oft there
> Where most it promises; and oft it hits
> Where hope is coldest—   II. i

The cure she is offering is something of a quite different order from the "labouring art" of the congregated college of physicians. So much was hinted at in the preceding act. We remember her use of the word "sanctify" and it slips into place, both in the general symbolism that gathers round all the heroines (the quality they stand for is alone able to turn the course of tragedy), and in respect of her individual

rôle. She has the approval, perhaps even the mandate
of heaven to heal the king and to achieve her love. The
remedy she brings is not, in under-meaning, physical,
but spiritual. And therefore—in spite of his firm,
"Fare thee well, kind maid!"—she stands her ground
with the king, and replies:

> Inspired merit so by breath is barr'd:
> It is not so with Him that all things knows,
> As 'tis with us that square our guess by shows. . . .
> Dear sir, to my endeavours give consent;
> Of heaven, not me, make an experiment. II i

He is sufficiently shaken by this to enquire how long
the cure will take, and she answers:

> The great'st grace leading grace,
> Ere twice the horses of the sun shall bring
> Their fiery torcher his diurnal ring— II. i

She promises, in fact, that within two days he will be
divinely healed; or if he is not, she is willing that her
life should pay the forfeit:

> With vilest torture let my life be ended. II. i

The king is amazed, his obstinacy vanquished, and he
accepts:

> Methinks in thee some blessed spirit doth speak
> His powerful sound within an organ weak:
> And what impossibility would slay
> In common sense, sense saves another way.
> Thy life is dear; for all, that life can rate
> Worth name of life, in thee hath estimate,
> Youth, beauty, wisdom, courage, all
> That happiness and prime can happy call. . . .
> Sweet practiser, thy physic I will try,
> That ministers thine own death if I die. II. i

If she fails, she dies; but if she succeeds, the king promises that she shall wed any man she choses, provided that he is free to marry her and not of the blood royal.

If there is anything more in this scene than theatrical effect, it is certainly not realism. But when we set it against Shakespeare's allegorical patterns, as we have traced them in other plays, much of the design is seen to be familiar. It is his standard practice that heaven should be revealed through the heroine; and when it is—as we noticed in particular at the close of *As You Like It*—every knot of error is untied, the spirit shines through the flesh, and material problems are solved. Although Helena is said to have "skill infinite", what really heals the king is his own trust and participation, through her, in the beauty that is heaven—a sphere in which all relationships are made perfect by love. And it is this divine harmony, this cosmos—and not merely Helena's person—that Bertram will presently reject; but unless we see the allegory here, we shall miss the tragic import of his coming action.

The king, of course, is cured. And before we see him come in—dance in, as some producers stage it—the conversation between Lafeu and Parolles confirms all previous hints by a plain statement: the cure has not been brought about by medical art, it is miraculous. Divine power has been made manifest in Helena, or, as Lafeu puts it:

A showing of a heavenly effect in an earthly actor.

II. ii

And again I would stress that this is what always does happen when the heroine's true nature is revealed:

"heaven walks on earth"—Olivia; "Hymen from heaven brought her"—Rosalind; "heaven is where Juliet lives"; and so forth. The hero's union with the heroine also implies his knowledge and recognition of the sovereignty of love in himself, and the resolution of Shakespearean tragedy depends upon this principle. It is an absolute panacea. The clown, in the short scene preceding this, has said:

> I have an answer will serve all men.   II. ii

Shakespeare not infrequently announces a theme through his clowns that he will develop through his heroes. In healing the king, Helena gives the all-inclusive answer. And to be sure that we do not miss this point—that the spiritual solution is assumed to solve the whole problem of life—it is brought up again by Parolles:

> —great power, great transcendence: which should, indeed, give us a further use to be made than alone the recovery of the king—   II. iii

The happy king now enters—with Helena and a following of elegible young lords. The time has come for him to redeem his promise: she may pick her husband. Her choice, of course, falls on Bertram, to whom she says:

> I dare not say I take you; but I give
> Me and my service, ever—   II. iii

Bertram is horrified, and flatly rejects her. When the king presses him, he replies:

> I know her well:
> She had her breeding at my father's charge.
> A poor physician's daughter my wife! Disdain
> Rather corrupt me ever!   II. iii

We have now come to a point where recognition of the allegory is not only valuable in itself but necessary to an adequate response to the story. *All's Well that Ends Well* is generally considered to be an unsatisfactory play; and this is largely because, at this juncture, Shakespeare fails to guide the sympathies of the audience as decisively as he intended. We are meant to feel, here, that Bertram is utterly wrong: if we do not, we shall be unable to participate in Helena's subsequent acts and feelings with spontaneous concern, and that is indispensable to a compelling drama. But no present-day audience can react as the author wished, when the king commands:

> Why, then, young Bertram, take her; she's thy
> wife.
> BERTRAM: My wife, my liege! I shall beseech your
> highness,
> In such a business give me leave to use
> The help of mine own eyes.
> KING: Know'st thou not, Bertram,
> What she has done for me?
> BERTRAM: Yes, my good lord:
> But never hope to know why I should marry her.
> KING: Thou know'st she has raised me from my
> sickly bed.
> BERTRAM: But follows it, my lord, to bring me down
> Must answer for your raising?   II. iii

I think most spectators would agree that the king has now lost our sympathies entirely; that we are sorry for Helena, but feel she has handled the matter with a minimum of tact; and that Bertram has not only scored a point, but—and this is near-disaster—that he is the only sensible person on the stage. It is true that he becomes unnecessarily rude; but when we have blamed him fully for that, we still do not feel an enormity of offence. And when he is married to Helena, under royal duresse, most of us will grant that he has reason to complain.

This is a serious blemish. It cannot be doubted that Shakespeare wished us to feel that Helena and the king were right, and Bertram thoroughly wrong, because that conviction is necessary if we are to be fully committed to her cause hereafter. But the story in itself fails to carry our sympathies as he desired; and there is nothing that will do so, except a deep feeling for the allegory. I have pointed out before that whenever psychological analysis presents grave difficulties in Shakespeare, we should always look to the parable; and here, once again, it provides us with the pass-key to this scene, and to all that follows. What Bertram has rejected, allegorically speaking, is the principle of love in his life: and this is the only thing, according to Shakespeare's scheme, that can lead him to the true beauty, which is a destination divinely willed for man. To this extent, the king speaks for God, when he exclaims:

Check thy contempt:
Obey our will, which travails in thy good:
Believe not thy disdain—   II. iii

But Bertram turns his back on what is, in under-meaning, the road to paradise. In place of love, he chooses war, and later lust; and invariably in Shakespeare this is a sign-post to tragedy.

The marriage takes place, a mere husk of ritual. And Bertram sends his wife—unloved and unkissed—

straight back to his mother's house, while he, defying
the king's express command, absconds to the Italian
campaign. In the scene of their parting, Helena's full
humanity—which we had been in danger of losing
touch with—is beautifully restored. When Bertram
says curtly, "My haste is great. Farewell, hie home,"
her moment of hesitation is natural and moving. He
responds to it roughly:

> What would you have?
>
> HELENA: Something; and scarce so much: nothing,
>   indeed.
>   I would not tell you what I would, my lord: faith,
>   yes;
>   Strangers and foes do sunder and not kiss.   II. v

She is denied her kiss, and sent away. She does not
weep, but we know her grief. And our sympathy,
which she had almost lost by her success, is revived in
her sorrow.

*   *   *

I cannot agree with the critics who maintain that
Bertram's flight to the wars redounds to his honour.
In my opinion, true honour and true love are inseparable in Shakespeare. He is always concerned with the
distinction between the seeming and the true; but
both, to our confusion, are designated by a single
word. Love, honour, nobility—each can be either a
dead mask or a living face. Shakespeare does not use
such words loosely; but he leaves it to us to discover
in what sense they are being employed. There is much
talk of honour in connection with the Tuscan campaign—but is it semblance or reality? The third act in
Shakespeare habitually gives prominence to the dark

forces; and in this play, it opens with a speech by the
Duke of Florence to two young lords from France.
He says:

> —now you have heard
> The fundamental reasons of this war,
> Whose great decision hath much blood let forth
> And more thirsts after.

> FIRST LORD: Holy seems the quarrel
> Upon your Grace's part; black and fearful
> On the opposer.   III. i

To Shakespeare, this rejoinder is stuff and nonsense.
The King of France sets his standard of rightness here:
and he has refused to be implicated in this "braving
war". And also the emperor, "our cousin Austria", in
the first act, "prejudicates the business", and this point
is stressed. The king permits his young nobles, if
they wish, "to stand on either part"—an impartiality
which makes it plain that there is no question of a
"black and fearful" Siena against a "holy" Florence.
It is a quarrel in straws.

The young man who agrees with the Duke of
Florence exemplifies the comment of his own king on
younger spirits—

> —whose judgements are
> Mere fathers to their garments—   I. ii

The second, who refrains from passing an opinion, is
wiser when he says:

> —I have found
> Myself in my incertain grounds to fail
> As often as I guess'd.   III. i

To such as these, the campaign may be "a nursery", in
which they will discover—as Parolles does—the

difference between falsity and truth. But Bertram has been expressly forbidden to go. And in voicing the hope that he will inherit his father's "moral parts", the king significantly adds:

> —and his honour
> Clock to itself, knew the true minute when
> Exception bid him speak—   I. ii

If anything is certain, it is that Bertram's clock is striking wrong—both in honour and in love. In decamping to Italy, he is taking the advice of Parolles, who tells him to copy the lordlings who are going there:

> —and though the devil lead the measure, such
> are to be followed: after them—   II. i

Bertram does follow: and in so doing he is rejecting the king, the fount of true honour, and accepting Parolles, a fount of false honour. And this exactly parallels his rejection of love—Helena—and his substitution for it of "sick desires", which he later feels for Diana. It is a principle with Shakespeare that whenever the soul disowns its divine qualities, the diabolic take their place: and it is impossible, in the Shakespearean scheme, for Bertram to be false to love and faithful to honour simultaneously. In the message the countess sends to him in Florence, she is as much illustrating this general principle as speaking her own mind:

> I will entreat you, when you see my son,
> To tell him that his sword can never win
> The honour that he loses—   III. ii

True honour and true love, false honour and "sick

desires" are bracketed in pairs; and there is nothing whatever to be said in favour of Bertram's decision to go to Italy; it is a movement which, if left unchecked, will lead to tragedy.

* * *

Helena returns alone to Rousillon. Letters from Bertram arrive, in which he repudiates her utterly, and swears that he will never come home while she is there. The countess is greatly angered by this, and gives Helena her full support:

>   —he was my son;
> But I do wash his name out of my blood,
> And thou art all my child.   III. ii

To Helena, however, although she keeps her intentions secret, this situation is intolerable. Bertram had said in his letter, amongst other things, "Till I have no wife, I have nothing in France." And so she argues, in a fine soliloquy, that it is her fault that he has lost his home, and that the only way in which she can show her love is to vanish without trace:

>   I will be gone;
> My being here it is that holds thee hence:
> Shall I stay here to do't? no, no, although
> The air of paradise did fan the house,
> And angels officed all: I will be gone,
> That pitiful rumour may report my flight,
> To consolate thine ear, Come, night; end, day!
> For with the dark, poor thief, I'll steal away.
>   III. ii

We may notice here how aptly Bertram's conduct, and the consequences of it, exemplify Shakespeare's theory of tragedy. All his tragic heroes are shown to strike at the best thing in their own lives: and the outcome of the deed is their self-destruction. Macbeth murders his king, and Othello his wife. Lear and Leontes drive out their daughters. Brutus "was Caesar's angel". And Hamlet—whose complicated problem I have discussed elsewhere—is really in no better case. The bedrock of Shakespeare's theory is that the tragic hero is striking at himself.

Shakespeare did not write tragedies merely for the sake of his own wealth and glory. He had a deeply ethical intention as well: his aim is to lay bear the causes of man's tragedy in principle, and then to show how its course may be checked and its wounds healed. In the last analysis, the resolution is shown to rest on the acceptance by the hero of the sovereignty of love; but there is more than one avenue to this conclusion. The creative power of forgiveness is Shakespeare's favourite way—exhibited by Prospero and many others. Repentance, as shown by Leontes, may attain the desired end. And the willing self-sacrifice of love, of which the heroine is usually the symbol, is also a redemptive power.

We have noticed this third form of resolution in *The Two Gentlemen of Verona*, in which Julia serves her faithless lover in disguise, and restores their mutual happiness by her constancy. In *Measure for Measure*, the rejected Mariana is also indispensable to Angelo's redemption. We are to witness the same thing here. Since Bertram has failed himself, and shows no intention of repenting, only Helena's self-sacrifice can save him from disaster. This is Shakespearean logic; for

love is the great link between the soul and heaven,
Bertram has severed the link, and without her fidelity
it is unlikely to be repaired. This rests on a general
proposition; and the countess is used, once more, to
make clear its particular application. When she learns
that Helena has vanished, she exclaims:

> What angel shall
> Bless this unworthy husband? he cannot thrive
> Unless her prayers, whom heaven delights to hear
> And loves to grant, reprieve him from the wrath
> Of greatest justice.   III. iv

The allegory, therefore, is concerned with the healing
ministry of love, which Shakespeare always shows to be
superior to justice. Helena has been successful with
the king; but Bertram is a more difficult subject. In
both cases, however, there is miracle and magic at work.
As we noticed in the first act, when Bertram went to
court, Helena resolved to "sanctify" her mental image
of him. The prescription that cured the king was, she
said, "sanctified by the luckiest stars in heaven". And
now, in the letter she leaves to explain her disappear-
ance, she says:

> Bless him at home in peace, whilst I from far
>   His name with zealous fervour sanctify.   III. iv

The word is not one of Shakespeare's favourites, and
this triple repetition is striking. Even without the
theory of the ascent, it would be clear that love is to be
gradually raised, by will and effort, as Helena's first
soliloquy sketched out, from the visual to the spiritual.
Marsilian Platonism conceived the ascent in this
fashion; but Shakespeare also draws on the medieval

philosophy of love, and its influence is particularly noticeable here.

The first statement in Helena's letter is that she is going on a pilgrimage, and from this point she glides through the play in the disguise of a pilgrim; but more and more, from the background shadows, she controls the plot, and becomes a figure of power. She never reaches the shrine of Saint Jaques le Grand to which she was supposed to be going, because she sets out in the opposite direction. The pilgrimage is entirely symbolic.

The conception of love as pilgrimage has a literary history that reaches back at least as far as Dante. It is in the interwoven themes of love, pilgrimage and vision that the *Vita Nuova* ends: a conclusion that points on, of course, to the *Divine Comedy*, with its ultimate revelation of love as the moving power of the universe—

l' Amor che muove il sole e l' altre stelle.

The Dantean tradition blended smoothly with, and was supplemented by the Marsilian. Shakespeare is in alignment with both. And when we appreciate this great current of thought in his work his appertaining ideas seem to sweep forward with new strength.

Love in Shakespeare is an ascent, a pilgrimage, and sometimes a *via dolorosa;* but he is particularly fond of the metaphor of pilgrimage, no doubt because it was the most satisfactory dramatically. In *The Two Gentlemen of Verona*, Julia describes her journey to Proteus as a pilgrimage to Elysium. In his first conversation with Juliet—a passage made deliberately unnaturalistic to enhance its symbolic meaning—Romeo presents himself as a pilgrim. And the key to Shakespeare's thought on this is given by Ophelia in her song:

> How should I your true love know
> From another one?
> By his cockle hat and staff,
> And his sandal shoon.

The metaphor of pilgrim is used consistently for the true lover; and in contradistinction to him is "another one"—whom Bertram will shortly exemplify. There is nothing arbitrary, therefore, in Helena's disguise: it is an important symbol to Shakespeare, and gathers the associations of a long tradition. The destination of the pilgrim is no shrine on earth, but the consummation of love in heaven; and as she gets nearer to this goal, Helena's dramatic importance grows, and her mysterious influence increases.

The plot now begins to turn on the other important point in Bertram's letter to Helena:

> When thou canst get the ring upon my finger which never shall come off, and show me a child begotten of thy body that I am father to, then call me husband: but in such a "then" I write a "never".
> III. ii

The ring is an heirloom, which it would dishonour him to part with; and it seems impossible that the second condition should ever be met without his consent. But he allows it to be fulfilled—in ignorance. This event is clearly symbolic: it illustrates the theory that even in love's phase of blindness—that of shadow-worship— it is nevertheless unconsciously directed towards the true beauty. Ficino states the principle in its theological form. I am not suggesting that Shakespeare is following him deliberately—it is a question of a Renaissance attitude of mind; but it is pertinent to notice here what Ficino says:

> Beauty is a kind of force or light shining from God through everything—first through the Angelic Mind, second through the World Soul and all other souls, third through Nature, and fourth through Matter . . . whoever sees and loves the beauty in these four . . . sees the glow of God in them . . . and loves God himself.

It is a very long time, of course, before anyone is supposed to be aware of this ultimate fact: veil after veil must be successively withdrawn, and each disclosure is a new revelation.

Bertram is not only at the bottom of the ladder, he has turned his back on it. This is normal in Shakespeare. His lovers frequently begin by scoffing; then they feel the power of love, and pass through a period of bewilderment, usually chasing the wrong woman; and finally they recognize true beauty through the one who is—I suggest—their predestined companion. And this ultimate clear sight includes self-knowledge. I have discussed this pattern in a study of the early plays, and Bertram's career conforms to it. First, he rejects love altogether:

> Great Mars, I put myself into thy file:
> Make me but like my thoughts, and I shall prove
> A lover of thy drum, hater of love.   III. iv

But this blind arrogance leads to his utter humiliation. He is soon infatuated by Diana. He dishonourably parts with his family ring in the hope of winning her. And pleads abjectly:

> Stand no more off,
> But give thyself unto my sick desires. . . .
> Here, take my ring:
> My house, mine honour, yea, my life, be thine,
> And I'll be bid by thee.   IV. ii

And in conclusion we are meant to believe—although many will find it hard to credit—that he sees the true light in Helena. This sequence occurs frequently in Shakespeare.

The happy ending could not have been achieved, however, without the solidarity of Helena and Diana. We have noticed the dual-heroine device already; and these girls are a fresh example—"like coats in heraldry . . . crowned with one crest", "like Juno's swans . . . inseparable". They are not physically inseparable, and here they have a different background—as Silvia and Julia had; but they are united at a higher level by a shared ideal. In this respect, "Juno's swans" is an interesting simile, because of the queer fascination that the anagram held for contemporary minds. Ben Jonson makes great play with it:

> And see where Juno, whose great name
> Is UNIO in the anagram—

It seems rather silly to us, and more suited to a cross-word puzzle; but Jonson turns it beautifully to account by concluding that the powers that descend from Juno-Unio dance the heavenly order into life—

> Their measured steps, which only move
> About the harmonious sphere of love.[1]

This easily suggests the thought that the unity of "heaven" is fragmented upon earth, but that beings

[1] *The Masque of Hymen.*

who know their divine essence will move in mutual harmony, while those who do not, will turn the dance of life into a *mêlée*. It is one more argument in favour of self-knowledge, and is consonant with the higher unity of the pairs of heroines that we find in several of Shakespeare's plays. Without that unity, the plots would break down. If the heroines behave as rivals— which they do for a short while in *A Midsummer Night's Dream*—a happy outcome is impossible. And it would have been so here.

When the disguised Helena reaches Florence, she hears that Bertram is doing his utmost to—

> Corrupt the tender honour of a maid. III. v

And it is on Diana's response to these advances that the plot now turns. Had she acted as a rival, there would have been confusion. But she declares herself an ally, even before she knows to whom she is speaking, with the words, "I would he loved his wife." And at the close of the act, she says to Helena, "I am yours—" It is another clear case of Juno's swans.

This alliance makes it possible to meet the stipulations in Bertram's letter. Diana lets him think that she will accept him, and he gives her the ancestral ring. She makes silence and darkness a condition of their love-tryst, and Helena keeps it in her stead. Luckily this leads to a conception: so Helena now has his ring, and, in prospect, his child. From the realistic point of view, it seems unlikely that this expedient would have been successful. But it appealed to Shakespeare, and in *Measure for Measure*, of course, he uses it again. This partiality probably comes from its aptness to the

parable. Although it may be said of the lover at this
stage, "Blind is his love and best befits the dark", none
the less, he is being guided unawares, by a power or
person he does not recognize, towards true fulfilment.
When Bertram thinks Diana is yielding, he exclaims:

A heaven on earth I have won by wooing thee.

IV. iii

Although based on false assumptions, this conclusion
is sound. It would seem to be a part of the theory that
the attaining of heaven comes through the union of
companion souls. If this appears too romantic to be
serious, we may recall that in Ficino's view, the first
dawning of creation, the turning of the Angelic Mind
to God, is very like a love-affair; and in any interpretation of Renaissance thought, it is well to bear the
doctrine of correspondences in mind.

* * *

There is no need to follow all the twists and turns of
the fifth act, which eventuate in Helena's triumph. The
nature of her victory—a living participation in true
beauty for herself and Bertram—and the means of
achieving it—constancy to love severely tested—are
now clear enough. But we may briefly notice how the
gaining of self-knowledge, a concomitant of the ascent
which Shakespeare never leaves out, is vividly presented
in Bertram and Parolles.

There is always a particular defect in the souls of
Shakespeare's tragic heroes, which lays them open to
some special kind of temptation. And the character
who tempts the hero to some extent personifies this:
if there were not a close inner correspondence between

hero and tempter, the temptation would have no effect—indeed, it would not exist. Parolles stands for false military glory: and this is equally the idol of Bertram's imagination, which Parolles stimulates him to worship. We have already seen that the King of France, in the first two acts, sets the standard of honour that Bertram should have observed: Parolles lures him successfully with its simulacrum:

> To the wars, my boy, to the wars!
> He wears his honour in a box unseen,
> That hugs his kicky-wicky here at home,
> Spending his manly marrow in her arms,
> Which should sustain the bound and high curvet
> Of Mars's fiery steed. To other regions
> France is a stable; we that dwell in't jades;
> Therefore, to the wars!

BERTRAM: It shall be so: I'll send her to my
house— II. iii

"Her", of course, is Helena—a "kicky-wicky" to Parolles, and the symbol of pure love to Shakespeare. Allegorically, therefore, the showing-up of Parolles is a logical preliminary to Bertram's own awakening. So close is the inner relationship between them, that Bertram is included—to his intense discomfiture—in Parolles' confession. And there is an obvious double-meaning in the comment of one of those who extorted the confession:

> A' will betray us all unto our selves. IV. i

In the fifth act, Bertram himself is subjected to a comparable exposure; and all these episodes (Act IV, scenes i and iii, and Act V, scene iii) develop a single theme—the stripping away of falsity and disguise from

the self. It is a most painful process, during which
every shred of adventitious dignity is lost; but it is not
mere punishment, and still less is it cruelty. Up to a
point, Shakespeare is merciless. Parolles is shown to be
a cowardly traitor and Bertram a contemptible cad.
But just when we are about to turn away from both in
disgust, Shakespeare re-illuminates them with a
brilliant shaft of insight: we are shown that all this
disgrace is but an accumulation of dirt, and beneath
it is an immortal spirit. When Parolles is left alone,
after his utter humiliation, he says:

> Yet am I thankful: if my heart were great,
> 'Twould burst at this. Captain I'll be no more;
> But I will eat and drink, and sleep as soft
> As captain shall: simply the thing I am
> Shall make me live.   IV. iii

We are at once reminded of the confession, in *As You
Like It*, of the far more villainous Oliver:

> I do not shame
> To tell you what I was, since my conversion
> So sweetly tastes, being the thing I am.   IV. iii

And when Parolles continues:

> Rust, sword! cool, blushes! and, Parolles, live
> Safest in shame!   IV. iii

we may even feel it to be linked with one of the most
beautiful short scenes in Shakespeare, in which Juliet,
in *Measure for Measure*, bears public disgrace for her
fault, if fault we can feel it to be, with the words:

> I do repent me, as it is an evil,
> And take the shame with joy.   II. iii

With this background in mind, we shall find it

easier to look on Bertram's ignominy in the final scene in the way Shakespeare intended. It comes very near to being a rite of purification. There is a positive value in this shame. It is meant to raise the question, "Who would escape it, if the truth were known?" And the answer is, "No one." But this is not discouraging, because if the truth were known—all the truth—it would make us free.

Perhaps Christian humanism, or Marsilian Neo-Platonism is an adequate term for Shakespeare's philosophy; but there is a great deal of originality in it which no name should be permitted to blur. There is an evident debt to the Gospels, and also, one would think, to Plotinus. If Shakespeare did not know the relevant passages in Plotinus, then he re-invented their leading idea—that to the "ugly" and deluded soul, two appeals should be made, first, to point out to it the shame of the things it now honours, and, second, to remind it of its lofty race and rank. It seems to me more probable that he had read, at least, *Ennead*, I. vi. And it would not be requiring much, either of his Latin or of his curiosity, to assume that he was familiar with the *Symposium* and the *Phaedrus*. Personally, I should credit him with more; but my interpretation of the plays is not dependent on that supposition. I believe that I have imputed no philosophy to him in this book that *might* not have been derived from Castiglione, Spenser, the Gospels, and conversation with his friends.

Bertram and Helena are happily united at last; but as in the cases of Proteus and Julia, Oliver and Celia, it is difficult for the audience to suspend its disbelief, and feel satisfied that this marriage is more than a dramatic convention; and because the depths of the spirit have been sounded in this play, to end in the shallows is unpleasing. Having crossed an ocean, we do not wish to run aground on a sandbank, but to reach a port. I would suggest that if we accept the parable in Shakespeare, then in each of these instances—and in others—we do reach a port. Allegory opens a new perspective. And at the end of it we no longer find a conventional tableau of wedded bliss; but we see the rescue of the lost as the great work of love, and ultimately—as in Plato, Plotinus, Ficino, Castiglione, Michelangelo, and many more—the union of the soul with eternal beauty.

Chapter VIII

TROILUS AND CRESSIDA

ALL'S WELL THAT ENDS WELL,
Troilus and Cressida, Hamlet—this has long been
the accepted order of the plays, although it is often
challenged. If Shakespeare re-handled his work as
frequently and thoroughly as scholars now believe,
there is no single date for the versions we have of them;
and they can never be arranged in a simple succession.
It would be out of place here to embark on complex
and inconclusive arguments on dating; but it does
seem to me that the once-agreed sequence of these
three plays is psychologically sound—that is, valid
from the point of view of the expansion and development of Shakespeare's thought.

All's Well that Ends Well forms a not unreasonable
conclusion to the religious aspect of the comedies.
Hamlet certainly opens the great period of tragedy. And
Troilus and Cressida (it has been described as "a History
in which historical verisimilitude is openly set at
nought, a Comedy without genuine laughter, a
Tragedy without pathos") is a play of transition. I
suggest that it may be best understood as a prelude to
tragedy. The tragic themes are announced, but their
development lies in the future: a prelude, or, if the
metaphor be preferred, a portico to the temple of the
Furies.

If this order of the plays is accepted, it might prompt

a question which at first sounds trivial: Why, in *All's Well that Ends Well*, did Shakespeare change the name of the heroine to Helena? In his source story, from *The Decameron Nights*,[1] her name is Giletta. Giletta is a pleasant and unusual name, such as Shakespeare might have been expected to like; and its association with lilies makes it particularly apt to a heroine so linked with the courts of France and Florence, and so notable for her purity of purpose. Why, then, change it to the relatively commonplace and seemingly inapposite Helena?

We may first notice that, while he was writing about her, the story of Troy was vividly in Shakespeare's mind. There are several references to it. And when Lafeu, having introduced Helena to the King of France, retires with the remark, "I am Cressid's uncle, that dare leave two together," it is such a strained comparison that we cannot but suspect that the Trojan theme was so alive in Shakespeare's thoughts as to be obtrusive. This makes it seem more than ever likely that the plays are consecutive, and both of them contain a Helen. Even those who consider the Helena of *All's Well that Ends Well* to be over-rated will grant that she is intended to ring true throughout; and no one will deny that the Helen of *Troilus and Cressida* rings false.

A true Helen, specially so-named for this occasion, and a false Helen—their respective stories were engaging Shakespeare's imagination at the same time. It looks like a deliberate contrast; and if there is an inclusive idea to explain this, it might have been the

[1] III. ix.

legend that the real Helen never went to Troy. According to this account, which appears variously in Herodotus, Plato and Euripides, there were two Helens, or a divided one—an inviolate beauty, and its simulacrum. Had Shakespeare known this story, it would certainly have attracted him; because it would be hard to find a more arresting illustration in classical literature of his theory of the face and the mask, the substance and the shadow.

We have shown some grounds for supposing that he was acquainted with the *Phaedrus*. And there Socrates relates how Stesichorus was struck blind for reviling Helen—a blasphemy since she was the daughter of Zeus—but had his sight restored when he wrote a recantation, which began:

> False is that word of mine: the truth is that thou didst not embark in ships, nor ever go to the walls of Troy.

The legend crystallized in the *Helena* of Euripides, according to which only a phantom was stolen by Paris and became his paramour; the real Helen was spirited away by Hermes to a sanctuary in Egypt; and when the mystified Menelaus finds her there, she says:

> To the domains of Troy I never went:
> It was my image only.

What significance Erupides may have attached to this is beyond our discussion; but to Socrates, Helen was probably a symbol of the divine loveliness which cannot be defiled; and this would surely have been a precious gift to Shakespeare, for he always implies that the true beauty eludes concupiscence. Was his own conception of the contrasting Helens influenced by the classical

legend? To suggest that he knew Plato's remark on it
would not be audacious; but that he had heard of the
play of Euripides is a speculation; and it is probably
only coincidence that the last lines of the *Helena*—

> The gods perform what least we could expect,
> And oft the things for which we fondly hoped
> Come not to pass; but heaven still finds a clue
> To guide our steps in life's perplexing maze—[1]

have an odd resemblance to what Shakespeare's Helena
says to the King of France:

> Oft expectation fails, and most oft there
> Where most it promises; and oft it hits
> Where hope is coldest and despair most fits.   II. i

But in any review of the surprising dispensations
of providence, this is, perhaps, an unavoidable
observation.

One point emerges, however, which I should like to
stress: the view of the rape of Helen, and its consequences, that Homer has made universally familiar is
not the only one which has classical authority. In the
opinion of Plato and Euripides, the Trojan War was
fought for a phantom. And whether Shakespeare was
fully aware of this or not, his own attitude to it in
Troilus and Cressida is a near parallel. Even Troilus,
who later argues for the continuance of the war, first
speaks of it as fatuity.

> Peace, you ungracious clamours! peace, rude sounds!
> Fools on both sides! Helen must needs be fair,
> When with your blood you daily paint her thus.
> I cannot fight upon this argument;
> It is too starved a subject for my sword.   I. i

[1] M. Wodhull's translation.

Diomedes is more definite and more bitter:

> Hear me, Paris;
> For every false drop in her bawdy veins
> A Grecian's life hath sunk; for every scruple
> Of her contaminated carrion weight,
> A Trojan hath been slain—   IV. ii

And Thersites puts it in his characteristic way:

> Here is such patchery, such juggling and such knavery! All the argument is a cuckold and a whore: a good argument to draw emulous factions and to bleed to death upon. Now, the dry serpigo on the subject! and war and lechery confound all!   II. iii

Shakespeare's Helen is seeming-fair: but she is only a wraith of true beauty, or even the archetype of falsity. As such, she represents the antithesis of the heroines we have examined so far. And the relevance of *Troilus and Cressida* to our present subject is that of definition by contrast.

This has far-reaching consequences for the interpretation of the play, since it falsifies the values of the combatants on both sides. It is a condition of tragedy in Shakespeare that the hero should mistake the shadow for the substance. This leads him to that inversion of values—"the tragic inversion", I have termed it elsewhere—by reason of which it is conscience, as he supposes, that requires his crime: Brutus, Hamlet, Othello, Angelo, Leontes—in act or intention, "honourable murderers" all. They are in a condition in which their very virtues betray them:

> —for where an unclean mind carries virtuous qualities . . . they are virtues and traitors too.
> *A.W.E.W.* I. i

Uncleanness or unclearness of mind is the inescapable state of those who are following false shapes. This is not the classical road to tragedy; but it is Shakespeare's, and by no means his alone. It is an expression in dramatic terms of something that Ficino had clearly stated in the language of religion. For Ficino, since the soul is divine, it cannot be eternally damned; but it can experience hell. In the Marsilian view, God and heaven are the highest reality, and hell is the ultimate in illusion. Accordingly, he argues:

> He who has followed true things during life, attains the highest truth after death; he who has followed false things is tormented by delusion—[1]

This hell-state is a kind of *delirium tremens*, from which, after much suffering, sanity will be regained. Shakespeare does not show much interest in eschatology—he is concerned with heaven on earth and hell on earth; but with regard to these, he holds almost exactly the Marsilian position.

We have seen in the comedies that when the heroine is fully revealed and won, "heaven walks on earth". In the tragedies we find the opposite: the heroine is lost, and hell is let loose, or, as Othello tersely describes it, "Chaos is come again."

These threads are woven into *Troilus and Cressida*. It is a play in which everyone is fighting for a shadow, and in which the heroine is ultimately lost. And I therefore suggest that we are intended to see the fifth

---

[1] "*Et sicut eum qui in vita veris incubuit, post mortem summa veritate potiri, sic eum qui falsa sectatus est, fallacia extrema torqueri, ut ille rebus veris oblectetur, hic falsis vexitur simulachris.*" *Theologia Platonica*, Book xviii, chap. x.

act as the diametrical opposite of the revealing of heaven: it is the unleashing of the powers of hell. But in this play they are not fully deployed. It is a prelude to the doom of Troy, the doom of the Greeks and to the tremendous tragic dooms that Shakespeare was intending to unfold. And it also gives us Shakespeare's explanation of why these calamities occur, in an ethical theory of crystalline rationality.

* * *

I pointed out in *The Shakespearean Ethic* that the tragic crime is never committed in Shakespeare until the hero has lost self-sovereignty. Chaos in the soul is his pre-requisite of tragedy; and the converse is also true. This implies a philosophy of order—both within and without; and when we have realized that this is one of Shakespeare's fundamental ideas, we find it in all his plays. Nowhere, however, is it stated more explicitly than in *Troilus and Cressida*, and nowhere is the dire outcome of its violation made more plain.

The subject is introduced by Ulysses, in the famous speech which explains the failure of the Greeks to capture Troy; and it is then illustrated by an analysis of the inner confusion of almost every character. But before we consider the theory that Shakespeare imputes to Ulysses, it is important to recognize that it derives from—or, at the least, had already been propounded in—the same Italian Neo-Platonic sources that enriched him with many other ideas. In his commentary on Benivieni's *Canzona dello Amore Celeste et Divino*. Pico della Mirandola had said[1]:

[1] Translated by Thomas Stanley as, *A Platonick Discourse upon Love*, ed. E. G. Gardner, 1914, The Humanist's Library, vol. VII.

The chief order established by divine Wisdom in created things is, that every inferiour Nature be immediately governed by the superiour; whom whilst it obeys, it is guarded from all ill, and led without any obstruction to its determinate felicity; but if through too much affection to its own liberty, and desire to prefer the licentious life before the profitable, it rebel from the superiour nature, it falls into a double inconvenience. First, like a ship given over by the Pilot, it lights sometimes upon one Rock, sometimes on another, without hope of reaching the Port. Secondly, it loseth the command it had over the Natures subjected to it, as it hath deprived its superior of his. . . .

The same order is the lesser World, our Soul: the inferiour faculties are directed by the superiour, whom following they erre not. The imaginative corrects the mistakes of the outward sense: Reason is illuminated by the Intellect, nor do we at any time miscarry, but when the Imaginative will not give credit to Reason, or Reason confident of it self, resists the Intellect. In the desiderative, the Appetite is govern'd by the Rational, the Rational by the Intellectual, which our Poet implyes, saying,

"Love whose hand guides my heart's strict
    reins."

. . . In every well order'd Soul the Appetite is govern'd by Intellectual Love; implyed by the Metaphore of Reines borrowed from Plato in his *Phaedrus*.

Pico wrote that about 1487, and although Stanley's translation did not appear until 1651, his ideas were well known in Shakespeare's time. The second paragraph, in particular, helps us to understand why Shakespeare thought of the human soul as "like to a little kingdom"; and why, when there is an insurrection there—a pre-condition of tragedy—what is assumed to be taking place is the usurpation, by some inferior power, of the throne that rightly belongs to Love.

Like many others, Shakespeare carried the doctrine of correspondences too far; and in the histories, which are his study of the soul of England, it shows signs of strain. But the broad strokes of analogy are most revealing there. When we set the words of Philip the Bastard, at the close of *King John*:

Nought shall make us rue,
If England to itself do rest but true—

beside those of Polonius:

This above all: to thine own self be true—   *H*. I. iii

we have a clue to something much more fundamental than rhetoric; something, moreover, that should not be confused with the national personifications that still feebly survive. If followed to the end, the clue leads us to a theory of universal order—assumed to descend from God and the "Hierarchy of Angels" right down to the physical elements. Pico has sketched this for us, and Ulysses adds some important details.

Inevitably, violation of this divine arrangement was thought to be impious, and the first step to calamity. It is because a king (whether he is personally worthy of it is a different question) has a place assigned to him in this order, that "divinity doth hedge a king". And that is what the King of France, in *All's Well that Ends Well*, means when he says: "I fill a place, I know't." The trouble with the Greeks, according to Ulysses, is that Agamemnon ought to fill that place, but he does not. He ought to be the

> —soul and only spirit
> In whom the tempers and the minds of all
> Should be shut up—   I. iii

But in point of fact, some of the other leaders, notably
Achilles, do not recognize his authority; and therefore
the Greek host, instead of being a solid battering-ram,
is a heap of splinters:

> —look, how many Grecian tents do stand
> Hollow upon this plain, so many hollow factions.
>   I. iii

And in spite of a seven-years siege, Troy still stands.

Ulysses would not have needed to make so long a
speech to explain this; but Shakespeare is taking the
opportunity to state a broad view of world-order, and
of the calamitous consequences of its disruption. This
forms an important part of his general theory of
tragedy—a theory which is completely non-Aristotel-
ian. If this conception of order does not derive from
Pico, it at any rate parallels his line of thought. But
Shakespeare's expression of it is characteristically
concrete. He says nothing about God and the angelic
hierarchy, although it is reasonable to infer that he had
them in mind as the supreme pattern: he points to
things with which everyone is familiar. First, there is
order in the heavens, of which Ulysses takes a
Ptolemaic view, although Shakespeare was quite
familiar with the Copernican:

> The heavens themselves, the planets, and this centre
> Observe degree, priority, and place,
> Insisture, course, proportion, season, form,
> Office and custom, in all line of order;
> And therefore is the glorious planet Sol
> In noble eminence enthroned and sphered. . . .

                    But when the planets
In evil mixture to disorder wander,
What plagues and what portents, what mutiny,
What raging of the sea, shaking of earth,
Commotion in the winds, frights, changes, horrors,
Divert and crack, rend and deracinate
The unity and married calm of states
Quite from their fixture! O, when degree is shaked,
Which is the ladder to all high designs,
The enterprise is sick.

He then turns to the social order; and as this has sometimes been described as mere feudalism, it may be
worth pointing out that it is not, in fact, static with
regard to individuals: there is a right way to climb the
ladder—it is the rungs of the ladder, in Ulysses'
argument, that ought to be fixed:

                    How could communities,
Degrees in schools, and brotherhoods in cities,
Peaceful commerce from dividible shores,
The primogenitive and due of birth,
Prerogative of age, crowns, sceptres, laurels,
But by degree stand in authentic place?
Take but degree away, untune that string,
And hark what discord follows! each thing meets
In mere oppugnancy. . . .
Strength should be lord of imbecility,
And the rude son should strike his father dead;
Force should be right; or rather, right and wrong,
Between whose endless jar justice resides,
Should lose their names, and so should justice too.
Then everything includes itself in power,
Power into will, will into appetite;
And appetite, an universal wolf,
So double seconded with will and power,
Must make perforce an universal prey,

And last eat up himself. Great Agamemnon,
This chaos, when degree is suffocate,
Follows the choking.   I. iii

This does indeed carry us far beyond the present
context. The self-devouring wolf and chaos—it is
what the tragic hero in Shakespeare gradually makes
of himself and of his world. And his first step in doing
so is to lose the true sovereignty of his inner kingdom
—"the lesser world, our soul", as Pico calls it. Both
Shakespeare and Pico make it plain that the soul's
crown and throne must be yielded to Love. This is
because, in the view of Marsilian Platonism, the
universal order itself is the creation of divine love; and
the soul-pattern and the world-pattern, when both are
perfect, correspond. Ficino went further: he identifies
love with the will of God. The soul that yields utterly
to love is, therefore, accepting the sovereignty of
God.

I do not know whether Shakespeare was aware of
this conception and shared it; but it would have been a
logical climax to his thought. Except for Antony, all
his tragic heroes cast out love, violate the divine order
in their own souls, and are therefore in disaccord with
the divine will: the outcome, in the external world, is
chaos. Although this argument may not have been
derived directly from Ficino, it is so close to his position, that I suggest it is substantially the Marsilian
pattern in dramatic terms. This is not improbable,
since Ficino was undeniably a potent influence on every
manifestation of Renaissance art. In any case, there is
no question whatsoever of "a muddled philosophy" in
Shakespeare. He has a dramatic, even a romantic

theory of the world and of the human soul; but it is one, also, of the utmost coherence and sublimity.

In *Troilus and Cressida*, the tragic pattern is being sketched, and will become plainer when we consider the inner confusion of the main characters. So far, Ulysses has been concerned with the failure of the Greeks through "neglection of degree", and he winds up his speech by saying:

—to end a tale of length,
Troy in our weakness stands, not in her strength.

I. iii

Agamemnon accepts this view of the situation; but a spectator of the play—still more, a reader of it—cannot fail to wonder why, if the Greeks are in such confusion, the Trojans have not long ago driven them into the sea. What is wrong with Troy? Shakespeare's answer to this is that the great principle of order runs through the universe, and the Trojans have disrupted it at a different level—they have violated the moral order. They are fighting for a false ideal; and, therefore, their very virtues betray them. This brings us back to Helen as a symbol of falsity—a carefully contrived antithesis of those other heroines who are allegorical figures of true beauty.

The second scene of act two shows us the Trojan leaders in conclave. It is a skilful counterpoise to the council of the Greeks, with Hector taking the place of Ulysses as the expositor of error. The scene opens with a speech from the throne, Priam says:

After so many hours, lives, speeches spent,
Thus once again says Nestor from the Greeks:
"Deliver Helen, and all damage else—

As honour, loss of time, travail, expense,
Wounds, friends, and what else is dear that is
   consumed
In hot digestion of this cormorant war—
Shall be struck off." Hector, what say you to't?

II. ii

This is the first occasion—there is another to come—
on which Shakespeare is plainly saying that the war
could and should have ended in a peace with true
honour to both parties. The conflict is perpetuated, at
least on the Trojan side, by specious honour; and
Trojan honour has become specious, because it is in
the service of a false ideal. But Shakespeare's thought
far transcends the Graeco-Trojan squabble at this
point: this is a theme—the winnowing of the chaff
from the grain—that in some form or other he treats
in every play. Here it is Hector, in his main argument,
who stands for true honour, as the king did in *All's
Well that Ends Well;* and Troilus, although a much
finer character than Bertram in other respects, is
dazzled, as he was, by a meretricious glitter. Hector
now answers Priam:

Let Helen go.

Since the first sword was drawn about this question,
Every tithe-soul 'mongst many thousand dismes
Hath been as dear as Helen—I mean, of ours.
If we have lost so many tenths of ours
To guard a thing not ours, nor worth to us—
Had it our name—the value of one ten,
What merit's in that reason which denies
The yielding of her up?

II. ii

This goes to the heart of the argument as Shakespeare
invariably unfolds it: sacrifice there must be in life;

175

but it is essential to ask, and with the utmost clarity to know, on what altar it is being offered. Many times we have seen an erring character redeemed by the self-giving of another, and the Shakespearean position is not in doubt: right and effective sacrifice is always on the altar of love—made, that is, to a supreme value. Hector uncovers the face of Shakespearean honour, but Troilus can see no deeper than the mask, and answers:

> Fie, fie, my brother!
> Weigh you the worth and honour of a king
> So great as our dread father in a scale
> Of common ounces?   II. ii

We cannot fail to notice the semantic shift: Hector spoke of the sacrifice of souls, Troilus has turned them into common ounces. He has not done this deliberately; but he is simply incapable—as Shakespeare carefully shows many of his characters to be—of the insight that can pierce to the soul of things. The trappings and the suits are all that he can see—in this scene, at any rate—and therefore they are all that he can value; but to Shakespeare, these are mere shadows and imaginings. Troilus cannot even appreciate reason, which the Neo-Platonists rated one degree lower than the soul-values for which Hector stands; and when Helenus supports Hector on rational grounds, Troilus replies:

> Nay, if we talk of reason,
> Let's shut our gates and sleep. Manhood and honour
> Should have hare-hearts, would they but fat their
>   thoughts
> With this cramm'd reason—   II. ii

Since the unreason of Troilus is conducing to disaster, this exchange may have relevance to the passage already quoted from Pico: ". . . nor do we at any time miscarry, but when the Imaginative will not give credit to Reason . . ." Troilus illustrates that; but Hector sides with Helenus, and says:

> Brother, she's not worth what she doth cost
> The keeping.

To which Troilus replies:

> What's aught, but as 'tis valued?   II. ii

This is to make value dependent on imagination instead of on reality—an error which Pico explains theoretically, and which constitutes the tragic blindness of so many characters in Shakespeare. Hector's answer brings the theory and the dramatic illustration into luminous conjunction:

> But value dwells not in particular will;
> It holds his estimate and dignity
> As well wherein 'tis precious of itself
> As in the prizer. 'Tis mad idolatry
> To make the service greater than the god—
>   II. ii

Again, Hector is revealing the soul of the situation. The service, virtue and sacrifice of Troy, all her noblest attributes, are being offered on the altar of a false divinity. As the Greeks have violated one sphere of order, so the Trojans have violated another: and the outcome will be calamity to both. Shakespeare, of course, relies on the sense of general doom impending, which the familiar story stirs in the audience throughout. And what he is striving to do is to explain, by an ethical theory, why this tragedy must occur. If we suppose his aim to be limited to the writing of a good play, we miss what is most deeply significant here— that he is wrestling with the dark and perennial problem of man's mutual destruction. This theme of horror, the self-slaughter of humanity, haunts him in *Hamlet*, in which the thought of race-suicide is closely interwoven with Hamlet's personal preoccupation with death. And in *King Lear*, he seems almost to despair:

> It will come,
> Humanity must perforce prey on itself
> Like monsters of the deep.   IV. ii

It is impossible to understand Shakespeare if we insist on believing that his main ambition was confined to the theatre. I doubt if anyone has been more sincerely and passionately concerned with the real state of man —his divine possibilities and his diabolical propensions. Both, of course, provide dramatic opportunities which Shakespeare exploits to the full; but behind the show-man there is always the thinker; and the more we analyse his thoughts, the more logically coherent they appear. He is attempting to show us the causes of tragedy, for no lesser reason than our salvation. One illustration of many is the doom of Troy. Hector, the man of true honour, and Helenus, the priest, have given us reasons; and now Cassandra, the inspired, gives us prophesy:

> Cry, Trojans, cry! lend me ten thousand eyes,
> And I will fill them with prophetic tears.

.   .   .   .   .

Troy must not be, nor goodly Illion stand;
Our firebrand brother, Paris, burns us all.
Cry, Trojans, cry! a Helen and a woe:
Cry, cry! Troy burns, or else let Helen go.   II. ii

This triple alliance—true warrior, priest, and prophetess—is a combination of tremendous power. And it
points to one thing: Helen is the symbol of a false
ideal. The love of Paris is "besotted", the honour of
Troilus is falsified, because they are being offered to a
phantom. And it is to be inferred that if the Greeks and
Trojans recognized the divine ideal—the true beauty,
the true honour—the war would immediately end.
After Cassandra's sooth-warning, Hector speaks again:

Now, youthful Troilus, do not these high strains
Of divination in our sister work
Some touches of remorse, or is your blood
So madly hot that no discourse of reason,
Nor fear of bad success in a bad cause,
Can qualify the same?   II. ii

It is a poignant situation. There is so much good in
"youthful Troilus". The blindness of inexperience is a
large part of his failing; he needs time to mature. But
the tragedy is closing in, and time will not be granted.
He is really far superior to Proteus or Bertram; but the
constant love of the heroine, which saved them, is
denied to him. Again, this points to the idea that
heaven may shine through the heroine, so that she
becomes a saving grace: and when she does, the
proviso, which precedes the lines quoted from *King
Lear*, may be met:

If that the heavens do not their visible spirits
Send quickly down to tame these vile offences,
It will come—   IV. ii

Heroines like Julia and Helena, who are willing to bear love's cross of sacrifice, *are* the visible spirits of heaven, and they do avert the tragic doom. But in this play, Cressida is as weak as everyone else, and her inconstancy adds only to the flames.

Hector, Helenus and Cassandra are now ranged against Troilus and Paris—the one group rejecting and the other supporting Helen as an ideal to live and die for. Priam, "our dread father"—who ought, like Agamemnon, to have exerted the true authority of kingship—is too physically and morally feeble to be anything but pathetic. Troilus and Paris remain unalterably hallucinated; and Hector addresses them in a last appeal. This speech, which is parallel or complementary to that of Ulysses, makes it quite plain that violation of the moral order is the weakness of Troy. It may be thought out of character for a warrior to be so philosophical; but if that is so, it merely underlines the fact that Shakespeare himself is propounding a theory that he wishes us to understand:

> Paris and Troilus, you have both said well,
> And on the cause and question now in hand
> Have glozed—but superficially; not much
> Unlike young men, whom Aristotle thought
> Unfit to hear moral philosophy.
> The reasons you allege do more conduce
> To the hot passion of distempered blood
> Than to make up a free determination
> 'Twixt right and wrong: for pleasure and revenge
> Have ears more deaf than adders to the voice
> Of any true decision. Nature craves
> All dues be rendered to their owners: now,
> What nearer debt in all humanity

Than wife is to the husband? If this law
Of nature be corrupted through affection,
And that great minds, of partial indulgence
To their benumbed wills, resist the same,
There is a law in each well-order'd nation
To curb those raging appetites that are
Most disobedient and refractory.
If Helen then be wife to Sparta's king,
As it is known she is, these moral laws
Of nature and of nations speak aloud
To have her back returned. Thus to persist
In doing wrong extenuates not wrong,
But makes it much more heavy. Hector's opinion
Is this in way of truth.   II. ii

It seems surprising, in face of such speeches as this—
and it is not a lone or outstanding example—that
there should be a school of criticism that soberly
ponders the query: "Did Shakespeare think about
anything at all?" How shall thinking be defined, if
this is thoughtless?

The Neo-Platonic pattern that we found in Ficino,
Pico and the oration of Ulysses is being carefully
filled out into a picture of all-embracing order. This
is not conceived by any of our authorities as arbitrary
or irksome; because, if it were lived, it would be a
divine harmony, and the achievement of the heart's
most deep desire. Why, then, is it rejected? According
to the Shakespearean argument, it is rejected because
man is not true to himself; and he is not true to
himself because he does not know himself and the
secret of his well-being. He mistakes the mask for the
face, the false Helen for the true, the shadow for the
substance: the metaphors are many, but *delusion* lies

181

at the core of Shakespearean tragedy, as for Ficino it was the effective cause of hell. Hector supplies a sad example. Having said so much that is noble, he is yet unable—like Hamlet—to be true to the highest that he knows. The exalting in the soul of a specious value, an action of vast import in the tragedies to come, is shown to us in five lines when Hector says:

> Yet, ne'ertheless,
> My sprightly bretheren, I propend to you
> In resolution to keep Helen still;
> For 'tis a cause that hath no mean dependence
> Upon our joint and several dignities.   II. ii

The renouncing of what is, in Shakespeare's conception, the hero's spiritual self for his superficial self is of fundamental importance. By doing this, the lordship of the soul is lost. The divine harmony and order within become discord and insurrection, and there is consequential chaos in the outer world. To grasp Shakespeare's meaning here is immeasurably to enhance the dramatic impact of his plays. It is human history, not merely the fortunes of one character, that is being debated in the great soliloquies. But it is not easy for us to feel this, because it is so different from our accepted view of life. It is habitual to most of us to envisage man, like everything else, as the product of environment; but to experience the full power of Shakespeare's drama we must suspend this modern thought and participate imaginatively in his: he conceives the soul as antecedent to its environment, determinant and creative.

Hector's apostasy—for the last lines of his speech are nothing less—is a spiritual abdication. But he remains nearer to the divine order than anyone else in the play; and his encounter with Ajax is another scene in which he brings the action, by reason and true honour, almost to the brink of peace.

Having given us an outline of the great pattern in the universe, Shakespeare now shows how it is shattered by the soul-state of individuals. We find most of them to be in the condition of Brutus, in the second act of *Julius Caesar*—riven with conflict, sovereignty usurped, a prey to hideous phantasma and the prefigurements of death. But Hector is of special importance. He is a symbol of the strength of Troy, both spiritual and physical. In Shakespeare, the spiritual power is always paramount; and if that has been sapped, neither valour, nor might, nor weapons, nor armour avail anything. Therefore Hector's spiritual defeat leads inexorably to his death and to the overthrow of Troy. If he had been true to himself, then, in Shakespeare's scheme, the tragedy could not have happened; for when the hero maintains his full integrity, and replies to the challenge of events as Florizel did—

> To this I am most constant,
> Though destiny say no—

he becomes a channel through which heavenly powers work; and to him, even fate must yield. Since the virtue of Troy is centred in Hector, this supreme victory might have been achieved through him. But he is unable to be constant to the truth he knows; he surrenders to the will of Paris and Troilus; and their will is committed to the service of an illusion. To this "mad idolatry"—his own words—he too submits,

turning to his young brother with the fateful words:
"I am yours—" In basic conception, this parallels
Othello's recognition of Iago: "Now art thou my
lieutenant." It is the tragic inversion.

To appreciate the sweep and power of Shakespeare's
thought here, we must compare this scene with the one
in which its consequences are worked out. In act five,
scene three, Hector leaves Troy for his last battle; and
he is shown to have become deaf and blind to the self-
same arguments and illustrations that he once urged on
Troilus. The truth that he formerly pointed out to
others is now invisible to himself: he is a victim of the
delusion that, in Marsilian theory, is the "reality" of
hell.

In this scene, all the inspired voices warn of the
general disaster that will follow Hector's fall. It may be
thought that the tragedy has already passed the point of
no return; but however that may be, as a demonstration
of Shakespearean principles, the way in which this
scene is shown to grow out of the earlier one is impressive. Hector's wife, the one constant woman in the
play, speaks first:

> When was my lord so much ungently temper'd,
> To stop his ears against admonishment?
> Unarm, unarm, and do not fight to-day.   V. iii

Hector, whose disposition is usually so gentle, dismisses
her with a threat. It is a significant opening action here,
because the rejection of love's guidance is a part of the
tragic madness; it is almost a Shakespearean ritual, and
Hector confirms it with a vow:

> By all the everlasting gods, I'll go!   V. iii

Cassandra now enters, and in her rôle of prophetess, solemnizes the premonitions of Andromache. Hector's retort is to command that his trumpet shall sound. Then Cassandra pleads with him:

> No notes of sally, for the heavens, sweet brother.
> V. iii

At other fateful moments in Shakespeare, there is delivered a message, a command even, from the spirit to the passions; and this the tragic hero always disobeys. So Hector answers:

> Be gone, I say. The gods have heard me swear.
> V. iii

The guidance of love and divination having been rejected, Cassandra offers reason:

> The gods are deaf to hot and peevish vows:
> They are polluted offerings—
>
> .   .   .   .
>
> It is the purpose that makes strong the vow;
> But vows to every purpose must not hold.
> Unarm, sweet Hector.   V. iii

This is precisely the point that he himself had put so forcefully to Troilus:

> —'tis mad idolatry
> To make the service greater than the god.
> II. ii

The virtue is not in the performance of the vow, but in its nature: even the best qualities, when in the service of delusion, are "fair fruit in an unwholesome dish". In his former state of lucidity this had been Hector's own argument, but he cannot appreciate it now. "I am

yours——", he said to Troilus; and although this is never
entirely the case (he rebukes Troilus still with, "Fie,
savage, fie!"), it has been so far realized that he replies
to Cassandra in the same spirit in which Troilus once
answered him:

> Hold you still, I say;
> Mine honour holds the weather of my fate. V. iii

The fruit is fair but the dish is damnable. This honour
in false service is leading not merely to personal, but to
national ruin. Hector is the pillar of Troy; and therefore Cassandra turns in pleading and in prophesy to the
king:

> Lay hold upon him, Priam, hold him fast;
> He is thy crutch; now if thou lose thy stay,
> Thou on him leaning, and all Troy on thee,
> Fall all together.

> PRIAM   Come, Hector, come, go back.
> Thy wife hath dreamed; thy mother hath seen
>   visions;
> Cassandra doth foresee; and I myself
> Am like a prophet suddenly enrapt,
> To tell thee that this day is ominous;
> Therefore, come back.   V. iii

Again, Shakespeare has marshalled his characters into
two groups—the one speaking for light and the other
for darkness. Hector has changed sides: and this is the
crux of the matter, in regard to the doom of Troy. But
the conjunction of the forces of light is even more
impressive than before: wife, mother, father and king,
sister and prophetess—each figure charged with vast
symbolic import. To defy them all is to fall like Lucifer.
Priam repeats:

> —thou shalt not go.

And Hector answers:

> I must not break my faith.   V. iii

Faith to whom? faith in what? These are the re-echoing questions. Hector goes. And as Shakespeare stages it, he is not even slain in battle—he is murdered. His sister will be raped, his city burned, his countrymen killed or scattered. A sacrifice, indeed; and heroically done, no doubt; but on what altar is it offered? Cassandra's parting words go straight to the point:

> Farewell: yet, soft! Hector, I take my leave:
> Thou dost thyself and all our Troy deceive.   V. iii

Falsity, in this play, is by no means confined to poor Cressida, to whom the label has in perpetuity been tied; incomparably the more important example—apart from the merely symbolic Helen—is the compromised nobility of Hector. The destruction of a nation stems from that. And as Shakespeare presents the same tragic inversion in other plays, he no doubt thought the moral to have perennial validity.

Here and elsewhere his emphasis falls on the individual soul as the determining factor in history. The divine order must be realized in the inner kingdom, before society can be set right. Love, self-knowledge, spiritual insight—these must come first: perhaps they are really one, the one thing that is supremely needful.

Like that of most great Renaissance artists, Shakespeare's philosophy is mainly Marsilian Platonism; but the intuition of an ultimate order, and the need for its manifestation in human affairs is a world-wide theme; and Shakespeare's presentation of it is often surprisingly consonant with Oriental thought. The famous opening section of *The Great Learning* is a case in point. In this, the Confucian theory of a perfect society revolves, like a wheel on its hub, about the central requirement of the self brought into harmony by insight:

> With the mind right the individual self comes into flower. With the self in flower the family becomes an ordered harmony. With the families ordered harmonies the state is efficiently governed. With states efficiently governed the Great Society is at peace. Thus from the Son of Heaven down to the common people there is unity in this; that for everybody the bringing of the individual self to flower is to be taken as the root. Since that is so, for the root to be out of order and the branches to be in order is an impossibility.[1]

Shakespeare would have agreed with that. His own metaphors relate rather to the sovereignty than to the blossoming of the self, but there is no essential difference. When the "golden flower" opens, an imperial faculty is revealed "in the purple hall of the city of jade"—that is, in the inmost recesses of the mind; and this is "the ruler" who must be enthroned. There is agreement that the condition of society depends on whether the individual knows or does not know this divinity within, on whether there is cosmos or chaos in himself.

In Shakespearean tragedy we see the objectification of an inward tumult, of which self-ignorance is the prime cause. This soul-state of the characters is always laid bare, but in *Troilus and Cressida* it is conspicuous. Pandarus says of Troilus:

[1] *The Great Learning and the Mean in Action*, translated by E. R. Hughes, 1942.

Himself! no, he's not himself: would a' were
    himself!   I. ii

Thersites says of Ajax:

    Ay, but that fool knows not himself.   II. i

And later we have his comic, scathing, but deeply
meaningful description of Ajax strutting round the
camp "asking for himself", finding nothing but a kind
of stuffed elephant, and then pausing to bite his lip—

    —as who would say, "There were wit in this head, an
    'twould out." And so there is; but it lies as coldly in
    him as fire in a flint, which will not show without
    knocking.   III. iii

To Achilles, Thersites says, "Thou picture of what
thou seemest—"; to Patroclus, "If I could ha' remembered a gilt counterfeit, thou wouldst not have slipped
out of my contemplation—"; and to himself, "How
now, Thersites! what, lost in the labyrinth of thy fury!"
But it is Ulysses who makes the most revealing of all
comments:

    Kingdom'd Achilles in commotion rages,
    And batters down himself.   II. iii

What lies immediately behind all this, I would again
suggest, is Ficino's *Letter to Humanity:* "Know thyself,
divine race clothed with a mortal garment!" The
thought is fundamental in all Shakespeare's plays. And
so we find, in *Troilus and Cressida*, that set in contrast to
the spiritual darkness and death-dealing rage, there are
flashes of illumination. When they come, the battle is
suspended; there is a glimpse of the unity of perfect
law, a recognition of the kinship between foes; and for
so long as the light remains,

             The issue is embracement.   IV. v

These are the moments of truth. Nothing prevents their prolongation except spiritual weakness. When the two noblest enemies meet, there is the sudden discovery of an oasis in the desert, which might—and Shakespeare surely means this very deeply—might have been extended till the whole wilderness should flower. Agamemnon says:

> What's past and what's to come is strew'd with
>   husks
> And formless ruin of oblivion;
> But in this extant moment, faith and troth,
> Strain'd purely from all hollow bias-drawing,
> Bids thee, with most divine integrity,
> From heart of very heart, great Hector, welcome.
>   IV. v

"Divine integrity"—if the characters were true to themselves, that would never be lost. But Shakespeare's purpose here is to show their failure, and the disintegration, individual and collective, that is the consequence. The love-story, to which we must now attend, is in this sense the counterpart of the siege-story; and we must banish all thought that Cressida is blameworthy in some pre-eminently sinful way: she fails in her own sphere—but so does everybody else, even "imperious Agamemnon".

*   *   *

It is a frequent complaint against *Troilus and Cressida* that its two stories are imperfectly connected; and it may well be that the love-story is the earlier, and that much of the siege-story has been grafted on to it. But none the less, when we look at the things that do bind them together, we find the intellectual link to be very strong. There is a theme on which the main events are strung: it is the breaking of faith with the ideal order —conformity with which would bring heaven on earth, and the disruption of which leads to chaos. All the principle characters know that, in their enlightened moments; and each of them presents to us a particular instance of a general apostasy. It does not matter whether the betrayal is said to be of heaven, of the true self, or of love; for all these appertain to the spirit, and constancy to any of them would lead to the ideal world of inviolable beauty.

Splendid qualities have been pointed out to us in Hector and in Agamemnon: and yet both of them are tragic failures, because they cannot keep faith with the best they know. The same is true of Cressida. I do not think Shakespeare intended us to see Cressida as "cheap stuff not only in what she says but in the way she says it"—as that, and nothing more. It is true that he never allows himself to like her, as Chaucer loved his Criseyde; and he gives her none of the qualities that make Criseyde so endearing. But Shakespeare's heroine was created for a purpose; and if we are to appreciate what that was, we must observe her good moments as clearly as her bad ones. She is, of course, a figure of inconstancy, and there is no question of white-washing her character; but it is necessary to take a balanced view of it; and as most critics have dwelt on her defects, it will be salutary to recall her better qualities.

It is clear that she loved Troilus while she was with him; and in Shakespeare's version of the story, he was her first lover. If she plays on his simplicity, which often verges on silliness, that is scarcely a crime, since women instinctively use what guile they can command in their dealings with men. She has moments of insight into her own frailty that are touching and honest; and while Troilus is still courting her, before any vows have been exchanged, she says:

> I have a kind of self resides with you,
> But an unkind self that itself will leave
> To be another's fool.   III. ii

There is no self-flattery in that: it is the truth. And, at the same time, Shakespeare is explaining her to us. She has two selves, and she will fail to live up to the better of them; but she is not unaware that the better exists. *Video meliora proboque, deteriora sequor*—it is the general confession in this play. And if we do not concede her sincerity here, we shall do worse than misjudge Cressida—a minor matter: we shall not experience the power of Shakespeare's main statement.

Why does Troilus lose Cressida? We are invited to notice that the fault is partly his. In the second act, Shakespeare so manipulated the plot that nearly the whole blame for the continuance of the war is laid on Troilus. There is no authority in his sources for doing so, the emphasis is his own; he intends to convey to us the impression that but for Troilus there would have been peace. Hector objected to the sacrifice of lives, on the grounds that the offering was to a worthless god. Troilus made light of that: but now, on the very same altar, he is compelled to sacrifice what he values most.

Cressida is to be sent to the Greeks in exchange for a Trojan prisoner; because her father, who had gone over to the Greek side some time before, has persuaded

Agamemnon to ask for her. The exchange is an incident in the war; and if there had been peace, it would not have occurred. Shakespeare always shows, though often very subtly, that a wrong action harms the doer. So now the deity of false honour, to whom Troilus had been willing to sacrifice others, is requiring something from him. And when Paris—his ally in the debate with Hector—tells him that Cressida must be given up, he says:

I'll bring her to the Grecian presently;
And to his hand when I deliver her,
Think it an altar, and thy brother Troilus
A priest, there offering to it his own heart.   IV. iii

This is neatly tied in with the sacrificial reference in the second act. Troilus is not without some blame for their separation, and the plot has been shaped to make us see this point.

He describes the offering as his own heart. But Cressida is the living victim. And critics who can see no good in her surely under-value the speech she makes when she learns what is about to happen. She is not trying to impress her lover—he is not there. She is alone with Pandarus, and can have no thought of aiming at effect when she says:

Time, force, and death,
Do to this body what extremes you can;
But the strong base and building of my love
Is as the very centre of the earth,
Drawing all things to it. I'll go in and weep.

IV. ii

Is she sincere? The poetry compels us to believe her. Shakespeare would not have written those lines if they had not been evoked by his own conception of a truth in Cressida concordant with them. It may also be pertinent to remember that this is the fourth act, in which the powers of light are usually displayed; and in the next scene but one we have Agamemnon's splendid speech to Hector. He speaks of "divine integrity": she, of the base of love, as the very centre, "drawing all things to it". They have not the strength to live their vision, but they both have it; and their speeches are complementary—each, in its respective story, being the moment of pure truth.

* * *

Three characters—Hector, Agamemnon, Cressida—speaking out of their flashes of self-insight, have proclaimed the ideal standard: their failure to maintain it is the failure of their world. That, I believe, is what Shakespeare intended; but no one has found this a clear and convincing play. We know of the carnage to come. It has no longer anything to do with the Olympians. It is being deliberately explained to us from the standpoint of humanist, or Marsilian ethics. And unconsciously, perhaps, we feel the need of more active human wickedness to account for such a doom. Shakespeare may have realized this himself; for in later tragedies, most notably in *Macbeth*, the requirement is fully met.

The yielding of a weak nature to temptation is not so much wicked as pitiful; and perhaps that is why the effect of Cressida's fall—at least on a contemporary audience—is not so powerful as it was meant to be. It is likely, however, that Shakespeare attributed what we should now consider an exaggerated importance to any sexual lapse, especially in a woman, and this element in itself may have been more disturbing to the Jacobeans. But although the spectator does not usually find *Troilus and Cressida* a satisfying play, the reader is in a more favourable position. On reflection, it is not in the least necessary that we should share all Shakespeare's judgements in order to appreciate the sweep of his vision of the whole. Many will not agree with the political implications of the speech of Ulysses—or of the theory of Confucius; but everyone may yet admire, and even feel exalted by the conception of cosmic harmony from which they both flow.

Shakespeare's ethic rests on his belief in law that *cannot* be circumvented; and the miraculous in his plays is never a suspension of this, but a demonstration of its finer workings. If there are certain ways to calamity and death, there are others, equally reliable, leading to immortal life. In the sonnets, Shakespeare declared war on Time—"Thy registers and thee I doth defy!" And in several of the plays, *Troilus and Cressida* is one, hostilities are renewed. His grand strategy, if I may so call it, is that Time shall be conquered by the realization of an eternal ideal: and it is to this end that there must be constancy and faith. Details of the perfect pattern are beyond scrutiny, and to quibble over these would be an impoverishment of thought; but integrity —to heaven, to self, and to love—is a wider concept; and this is not limited by its illustrations. What Shakespeare is insisting on, it seems to me, is that there must be this higher constancy if earth is to be attuned to heaven, and human relationships wrought to a harmony that Time can neither stale nor destroy. As an audience, belief is not required of us: all that is essential is that we should respond to this vision as a work of art, and appreciate the sublimity of his vast design.

What is tragic—in the Shakespearean sense—in *Troilus and Cressida*, is that the characters who see most deeply do realize the eternal value; for a moment, they are united with it; and then they snap the link. Hector saw the way of truth, Agamemnon knew divine integrity, Cressida touched the base and centre of eternal love: they had but to be constant to be perfect. But no one is constant: and perhaps the most searching comment on them all is the line of Pandarus:

> Fair prince, here is good broken music.   III. i

The music of heaven broken into discord—such a thought lies behind the outburst of Troilus after he has seen Cressida with Diomedes. This important speech is not naturalistic, not what any young man under the circumstances might have said; it is not an uprush of passion like that of Leontes—"goads, thorns, nettles, tails of wasps"; for beneath the foam of it, there is an argument, remote from the emotion of Troilus, in which Shakespeare's mind is working calmly.

The purpose of this thoughtful statement is to draw a parallel between what Cressida is doing and what the other characters have already done—breaking the contact between earth and heaven, which alone brings harmony to the affairs of men. Troilus cannot believe that she would do this, and in his anguish he reasons:

> If beauty have a soul, this is not she;
> If souls guide vows, if vows be sanctimonies,

> If sanctimony be the gods' delight,
> If there be rule in unity itself,
> This is not she.   V. ii

That is not an eruption of jealousy, it is an argument:
Cressida's primary inconstancy is not so much to her
lover as to "unity itself". She is going the way of all
Shakespeare's tragic heroes, whose first fault is to
betray, or to lose contact with, their own spiritual
nature, which ought to be the ruling faculty within
them. A splitting of the higher personality from the
lower—"self from self"—is the central notion. And so
Troilus continues:

> —this is, and is not, Cressid!
> Within my soul there doth conduce a fight
> Of this strange nature, that a thing inseperate
> Divides more wider than the sky and earth—   V. ii

This love-triangle, which superficially may seem rather
a petty one, is being linked with a cosmic theme.
Human destiny is being studied here; and the humanist
assumption is made, as always by Shakespeare, that
men and women are not pawns, but the responsible
possessors of decisive power. They have the world
they chose: and the decisions of Shakespeare's major
characters epitomize the choice of man. In this scene,
the universal drama is compressed into the soul of a
frail girl, and revealed in four blazing lines by the
lover she has betrayed:

> Instance, O instance! strong as Pluto's gates;
> Cressid is mine, tied with the bonds of heaven:
> Instance, O instance! strong as heaven itself;
> The bonds of heaven are slipp'd, dissolv'd, and
>   loos'd—

The dissolution of earth's bond with heaven is a concomitant of the tragic deed in Shakespeare; in fact it is a further way of stating, in more or less religious language, his definition of what tragedy is. Cressida has thus contributed her share—and for this she is neither more nor less to blame than anyone else —to a disintegration which will be completed with the slaughter of the Trojans and the scattering of the Greeks.

It must be admitted, however, that in the theatre, Shakespeare does not succeed here. In contrast with its symbolic immensity, the example seems too trivial. The disparity is too great for the audience to feel the fusion of fact and symbol; and so the horripilant moment, essential to stage-tragedy, is not achieved. When Macbeth determines to "cancel and tear up" the self-same "great bond", his speech brings a shudder of conviction. None the less, the bond of love—*nodus perpetuus et copula mundi*—has been loosened; and from this moment in *Troilus and Cressida*, the play is conceived as a portico to hell. For our understanding of Shakespeare, it is therefore a most helpful frontispiece to the great tragedies.

In Hector, we watch the dimming of the inner light in a soul of potential glory; and this goes a great way towards giving him tragic stature in the Shakespearean sense. But Cressida is a pathetic figure. If she had been driven to infidelity by some imperious passion, perhaps, she might have roused the audience into conceding her great guilt. But no woman ever gave a more feeble explanation of her fall:

Ah, poor our sex! this fault in us I find,
The error of our eye directs our mind:

What error leads must err; O, then conclude
Minds sway'd by eyes are full of turpitude.   V. ii

A more lame excuse for fornication, and a floppier exit
from the play, would be difficult to imagine. The
comment of Thersites, that her "mind is now turn'd
whore", helps a little. But no actor in the part of
Troilus could lift this incident convincingly, within a
couple of minutes, to a level of cosmic importance.
That, nevertheless, is what Shakespeare intended it to
have: and our present purpose is not to criticize, but
to understand.

Why then, in a work of such generally high intellectual quality, did he allow Cressida's farewell lines
to stand? I suggest that he did so because the whole
play is conceived within the frame of Marsilian theory,
and eyes—although in this context they are dramatically weak—are theoretically of great importance there.
On the one part, Marsilianism is concerned with a
divine order and hierarchy of the spirit—as expounded
in the passage quoted from Pico. On the other part, it
centres round the doctrine of the ascent: and the idea of
two kinds of sight, one turned outward and the other
inward, is indispensable here. While the mind relies on
the outer eye, it is led by shadows and full of turpitude:
when it uses the inner eye, it perceives the spiritual
truth and beauty. Platonists have expounded this by
various parables and metaphors. Shakespeare does so,
as we have noticed, in a way that is dramatic and
romantic—for him, it is love-sight that reveals "that
inmost faire".

Clearly, such vision will be conferred only by love of

an exceptional quality, and Cressida has herself defined what it must be: love that will challenge "time, force, and death", and draw all things to its centre. The heroines of the comedies, around whom Shakespeare has carefully gathered the imagery of "heaven", are assumed to possess and to inspire such a love; and in consequence, as allegorical figures, they not only show, but in a sense they are the celestial beauty. In their persons, Shakespeare wins his war against Time; because he unites them, and their heroes, with a value —"firmly stayd, upon the pillours of Eternity". By implication, he is using Plato's argument that love is both a longing for immortality and a means of becoming immortal.

Some critics, I suggest, have judged Cressida too harshly for failing to realize so tremendous an ideal— no one is constant to the spirit in this play; but she is linked with Helen to exemplify a particularly flagrant breach of faith. Whether Shakespeare was influenced by the legend of the two Helens is admittedly open to question; but Troilus does say that there are two Cressidas—and "Diomed's Cressida" is an empty husk. In her—and, I think, in Helen also—we are shown a severance of the lower self from the higher; and this is an allegory of the breaking of the bond between earth and heaven. What comes of that is worked out in the tragedies, and this play of transition is a preparation for them. But it is also helpful to an understanding of the comedies, because it presents the dark counterpart of their figure of light:

If beauty have a soul, this is not she.

Chapter IX

CONCLUSION

THE notion of a definitive criticism is a death-thought, which withers the mind that entertains it. A critic may be more guarded against prejudice, personal and collective, than other people, but he can never be safe from it; and the greatest critics of Shakespeare—Dryden, Johnson, Coleridge, Bradley —all reveal as much, perhaps even more, of themselves and their age as of their subject. This is something inevitable, which it would be pointless to deplore. The full meaning of a work of art—if that phrase itself is meaningful—is all that it can mean to everyone who has ever beheld it or ever will, and so it is continually expanding.

It is natural—and probably wise—to suspect the critic who pontificates. Nevertheless, it is a part of his duty to be clear. He is obliged to say that what he has found in the work he is exploring is distinctly *this*; but unless his aim is to kill—which sometimes it is—he should grant that it may mean also an undelimited *that*. In art, as in religion, everyone must build his own house of understanding; but it is spiritual suffocation to seal up the windows and the doors.

I have not at any time attempted to describe the whole Shakespearean edifice; and some of my readers have accordingly supposed that I undervalue the pure drama of the plays. This is not so. On the contrary, I have always assumed that anyone who cares for Shakespeare at all must appreciate him aesthetically; but it is a part of the critical problem that this experience may be so intense as to eclipse every other. I know this, because for many years I was able to respond to Shakespeare only as poet and dramatist. But there is something else: the drama rests on and expresses a philosophy of life. This deserves investigation in its own right; and to understand it—an aim I have pursued, but do not claim to have achieved—would be to expand and not to restrict appreciation.

In everything I have written on Shakespeare, my intention has always been to keep the doors wide open. If a dogmatic tone is sometimes heard, that is only a concession to clarity that to some extent, albeit regretfully, must be made. I believe Shakespeare had a lucid philosophy and a clear ethic; but theories of a muddled and mercenary Shakespeare have led to some excellent books. Even the comment of Bernard Shaw —"With the single exception of Homer, there is no eminent writer, not even Sir Walter Scott, whom I can despise so entirely as I despise Shakespeare when I measure my mind against his"—even this is of worth: to those who take their Shaw solemnly it is a warning, and to everyone else a delight. The more views of Shakespeare we have the better. I have attacked those of several writers, but I am grateful to them all— *Vivat doctorum felix industria!*

If in this book I have unduly emphasized Shakespeare's debt to a philosophic tradition, it is not at all because I disagree with those who look on him as "a great original". I should fully endorse the judgement of Kathleen Nott that the uniqueness of Shakespeare lies in his unsurpassed fusion of "action, image and thought". The only excuse I can offer for my over-stress on *thought* is that at the present time—as it seems to me—this is the direction in which the balance of criticism needs to be redressed.

If a clearly conceived philosophy is implicit, then it is by parable and allegory that it is expressed; and the recognition of this—I think—immensely enhances our enjoyment of the plays: it gives them a new dimension and a richness that has yet to be explored; it is a stimulating challenge to acting and production; and to the audience it reveals a drama beyond the theatre, written, as Coleridge so finely said, for the stage of the universal mind.

Since criticism, appreciation and interpretation are an ever-expanding sphere, few writers on Shakespeare —or on any major artist—are entirely consistent. I do not claim to be, although I believe that Shakespeare held and expressed consistent views. But if I were embarking, now, on a study of the tragedies, there is little that I should alter in my first book. The mystery plays, the tradition of the Rose, and Marsilianism are three among several blended elements that need to be separately explored. But living closely for a time with the comedies has given me—or so I feel—a better understanding of the tragedies: I see them now as an inevitable development of Shakespeare's thought; there may have been events in his personal life that helped to precipitate them; but he would have written them in any case. The comedies tell us what happens when earth's bond with heaven is made firm in the human soul: the tragedies show what takes place when it is not. All Shakespeare's plays are phrased and felt in terms of Christian humanism. But they are, in fact, a dramatic statement of perennial religion—that there *is* a cosmic harmony, and that to achieve conscious participation in it is the problem, the challenge, and the salvation of man.

I feel more than ever convinced that the tragic heroes are being tested against a perfect standard, and that the degree to which they fail the divine in themselves is the measure of their fall. And conversely, that the regenerating heroes are to be understood as attaining—or at any rate approaching—a state of superhumanity.

> *Cognosce teipsum, divinum genus mortali veste indutum!*[1]

Ficino's awakening thought stirred up the Renaissance mind. And when we place the great problem figures of Hamlet and Prospero—the one who failed, and the one who achieved—in relation to it, each of them is freshly illumined.

If it be accepted—and only a part of the evidence has been put forward in this book—that the heroine may be a symbol of the imperishable beauty, a vicereine of heaven upon earth, then the hero who wins her utterly could not be less than a figure of the divine man; for as Socrates observes of the soul that has completed the ascent of love, "He shall be called the friend of God: and if ever it is given to a man to put on immortality, it shall be given to him." It was not difficult

[1] See page 35.

for Christian thought to re-interpret this as the coming to maturity of a true child of God.

*   *   *

The revival of the Platonic vision in the Renaissance has, perhaps, a special fascination for our fragmented age. It was coincident with the disintegration of medievalism, it transcended the boundaries of religious dispute, and it did at least point towards a new concord and reconstruction. Shakespeare may possibly have felt this—if he shared the vision, as I think he did—when he made Hippolyta say, "But all the story of the night told over . . . grows to something of great constancy."

The constant thing, as I suggested at the beginning of this book, was beauty—the kind of beauty that is only to be achieved through love. For this reason, love was shown to be above the law. Since laws serve mainly to protect us from our fellow creatures, in a perfect society—as has often been remarked—there would be no laws, because there would be no need for any:

fungitur in vobis munere legis amor.

Perfect man in a perfect society—as I have tried to show in discussing *As You Like It*, that Marsilian ideal is the secret aspiration of Shakespearean comedy; it is visionary, of course, but it is splendid. And it would be a mistake to call it phantasy, because it rests on a proposition not easy to refute—that, finally, no power on earth will dominate the spirit.

Ficino's philosophy was also a faith; and, as always, when a faith becomes a fashion, there were many trivial minds to take it up. But the vision was also recorded in great works of art, and that is surely some encouragement to-day. Even in our own disconsolate century we have not ceased to look for unity, for the spirit, for the whole. Some sense of it is an ageless need.

> I find the whole in elusive fragments: let one be caught
> And profoundly known—that way, like a skeleton key, the part
> May unlock the intricate whole. What else is the work of art?[1]

Does the work of art provide such a key? Perhaps—in so far as it springs from the will to create and to reveal. But the pursuit of the whole, by whatever ways and means, is a natural propensity of the mind—we have no choice but to continue: yet reason is mistrustful of the spirit, sceptical of the value of its aim. The more we are aware of this inner debate, the more we shall admire, as it seems to me, that response of genius which is Plato's equation of ultimate experience with imperishable beauty. It is not—and perhaps there cannot be—a purely rational conclusion; but it is a recognition of the fact that, in the same way that it is the nature of mind to expand, so love, when it becomes conscious, cannot choose but set out on an ascending quest. Socrates asked the right question, What is the nature and the goal of love? And when the Platonic revival came, the intervening Christian centuries were able to add something vital to his reply: love was still to bring forth in beauty, but it was also, and perhaps chiefly, the utmost of self-giving. Ficino drew all this

[1] C. Day Lewis, *An Italian Visit*, Jonathan Cape, 1953.

CONCLUSION

together with a sure mind, and communicated his certainty to the artistic intelligence of his age. Michelangelo spoke for this—and certainly for Shakespeare —when he said that love turned his eyes to beauty, and beauty leads the soul to whatever heaven there may be:

I son colui che ne' prim anni tuoi
Gli occhi tuoi infermi volsi alla beltate
Che dalla terra al ciel vivo conduce.

APPENDIX I

Selected Stanzas from
An Hymne in Honour of Beautie

We have noticed that in one of his few direct references to living persons Shakespeare tells us of his love of Spenser's "deep conceit"—meaning, of course, the profundity of Spenser's ideas.[1] This gives a helpful clue to Shakespeare's own way of thinking; and since he habitually appropriated whatever he admired, it at once raises the question, In what form is Spenserian "conceit" incorporated in the plays?

In *Shakespeare and The Faerie Queene*[2]—a work I had not read until this book was finished—Professor A. F. Potts has thrown a great deal of light on this fascinating problem; and it will require some ingenuity on the part of those who are determined to deny parable and allegory in Shakespeare to explain away this important study. Since Professor Potts concentrates his attention on *The Faerie Queene*, he has assumed that Shakespeare's early plays owe nothing to Spenser. But *An Hymne in Honour of Love* and *An Hymne in Honour of Beautie* were, Spenser says, composed "in the greener times of my youth" and "many copies thereof were formerly scattered abroad". And I would suggest that it was, in particular, *An Hymne in Honour of Beautie*

---

[1] See above, page 12.
[2] Cornell University Press, 1958.

208

which stirred Shakespeare's imagination as a young man, and remained as a pervasive influence.

This hymn is of cardinal importance, because it neatly sums up, for English readers, the most dramatically valuable part of the doctrine of Florentine Neo-Platonism. Its derivation has been lucidly described by J. B. Fletcher in "Benivieni's Ode to Love and Spenser's Fowre Hymnes", *Modern Philology*, vol. viii, 1911; and R. W. Lee, "Castiglione's Influence on Spenser's Early Hymns", *Philological Quarterly*, vol. vii, 1928, may also be consulted in this connection; but I think that even the brief presentation of Marsilianism that has been attempted in this book will have been sufficient to show the provenance of Spenser's ideas. For convenience of reference, I reproduce below those stanzas that are particularly relevant to our enquiry.

16

For when the soule, the which derived was,
At first, out of that great immortall Spright,
By whom all live to love, whilome did pas
Down from the top of purest heavens hight
To be embodied here, it then tooke light
And lively spirits from that fayrest starre
Which lights the world forth from his firie carre.

17

Which powre retayning still or more or lesse,
When she in fleshly seede is eft enraced,
Through every part she doth the same impresse,
According as the heavens have her graced,
And frames her house, in which she will be placed,
Fit for her selfe, adorning it with spoyle
Of th'heavenly riches which she robd erewhyle.

19

So every spirit, as it is most pure,
And hath in it the more of heavenly light,
So it the fairer bodie doth procure
To habit in, and it more fairely dight
With chearful grace and amiable sight;
For of the soule the bodie forme doth take;
For soule is forme, and doth the bodie make.

21

Yet oft it falles that many a gentle mynd
Dwels in deformed tabernacle drownd,
Either by chaunce, against the course of kynd,
Or through unaptnesse in the substance fownd,
Which it assumed of some stubborne grownd,
That will not yield unto her formes direction,
But is perform'd with some foule imperfection.

All this is pure Marsilianism, and so is Spenser's
insistence that love is the active principle at work. As
we saw, love was said to arise at the dawn of creation,
and then at once—"it draws the Angelic Mind to
beauty, and a substance that was shapeless becomes
fair". In a comparable way, it is the mutual love
between embodied souls that reveals their inner beauty:

26

But gentle Love, that loiall is and trew,
Will more illumine your resplendent ray,
And add more brightnesse to your goodly hew,
From light of his pure fire; which, by like way
Kindled of yours, your likenesse doth display;
Like as two mirrours, by opposed reflection,
Doe both express the faces first impression.

27

Therefore, to make your beautie more appeare,
It you behoves to love, and forth to lay
That heavenly riches which in you ye beare,
That men the more admyre their fountaine may;
For else what booteth that celestiall ray,
If it in darkness be enshrined ever,
That it of loving eyes be vewed never?

In fine, the soul is born to do a definite work: it is to
re-shape the world into the likeness of heaven, and it
already possesses the heavenly pattern in its own self-
nature. I believe Shakespeare shared this view; and
that he was also in sympathy with the way in which
Spenser works out the theory of affinity into a precise
doctrine of souls who are pre-destined to love each
other, and between whom alone marriage on earth will
be true harmony:

28

But, in your choice of loves, this well advize,
That likest to your selves ye them select,
The which your forms first sourse may sympathize,
And with like beauties parts be inly deckt;
For if you loosely love without respect,
It is not love, but a discordant warre,
Whose unlike parts amongst themselves do iarre.

29

For love is a celestiall harmonie
Of likely harts composed of starres concent,
Which ioyne together in sweete sympathie,
To work each others ioy and true content,
Which they have harbourd since their first descent
Out of their heavenly bowres, where they did see
And know ech other here belov'd to bee.

30

Then wrong it were that any other twaine
Should in Loves gentle band combyned bee
Than those whom Heaven did at first ordaine,
And make out of one mould the more t'agree;
For all, that like the beautie which they see,
Straight do not love; for Love is not so light
As streight to burne at first beholders sight.

31

But they, which love indeede, looke otherwise,
With pure regard and spotlesse true intent,
Drawing out of the obiect of their eyes
A more refyned form, which they present
Unto their mind, voide of all blemishment;
Which it reducing to her first perfection,
Beholdeth free from fleshes frayle infection.

34

For lovers eyes more sharply sighted bee
Then other mens, and in deare loves delight
See more then any other eyes can see,
Through mutuall receipt of beames bright,
Which carrie privie message to the spright,
And to their eyes that inmost faire display,
As plaine as light discovers dawning day.

I think that almost every idea in the above stanzas that
is susceptible of dramatic presentation will be found to
have important echoes in Shakespeare.

APPENDIX II

Passages from Marsilio Ficino's Commentary
on the *Symposium*

As the Italian version of Ficino's Commentary on the *Symposium* can be consulted only in rare editions, it seemed necessary to include the original of my quotations. In some cases, where I thought it might be helpful, I have given a few lines more than I have translated. The first reference numeral is that of the page in this book where the quotation occurs, and those at the end of each passage relate to the speech and chapter in the edition from which my translations were made: *Sopra l'Amore o Vero Convito di Platone*, Firenze, 1594. This is not, of course, the first edition, but I found it the clearest of those that were available to me.

Fortunately, the Latin version of the Commentary, with an English translation by S. R. Jayne, is again obtainable,[1] after nearly four centuries of neglect. And I should like to express my agreement with the concluding sentences of Mr Jayne's introduction:

> But there is ample room for new and further work; and the first stone to be laid in the foundation for that work is a first-hand intimate knowledge of Ficino. Even this, as we have seen, is not enough, for Ficino must be understood, not only in his relation to Plato and Plotinus as philosophers in their own right, but as the central figure in a great

[1] University of Missouri Studies, vol. XIX, No. 1, 1944.

movement. Out of this movement sprang a persistent and powerful, if silent, force that made its way into English literature, determining more than is usually recognized the nature and quality of much of its poetry and prose. It is the hope of the present writer that the text and translation of Ficino's *Commentary* which follow may be of some slight service to those who aspire to follow this particular path of thought and truth.

I feel sure that this hope will be realized, because we cannot understand our own sixteenth century fully until we have explored this path. What is needed are not more books about Ficino (although an English translation of Giuseppe Saitta's brilliant study, *La Filosofia di Marsilio Ficino* would be very welcome), but competent translations of his own work. We owe a great debt to Mr Jayne for undertaking a part of this task. It seems strange that so many Latinists should be content to re-edit and re-translate classical texts that have been worked over for centuries, while exciting territory in the Renaissance remains almost virgin soil.

36   La Mente Angelica è il primo Mondo fatto da Dio: Il secondo è l'anima dell'Universo: Il terzo è tutto questo edificio, che noi veggiamo.   I. ii

37   . . . laquale essenzia, per ancora di forme privata vogliamo, che Caos certamente sia. E'l suo primo voltamento a Dio è il nascimento d'Amore: la infusione del Raggio, il nutrimento d'Amore: lo incendio che ne seguita, crescimento d'Amore si chiama. L'accostarsi a Dio è l'impeto d'Amore: la sua formazione è perfezione d'Amore, e l'adunamento di tutte le forme e Idee, i Latini chiamano Mondo, e i Greci Cosmo, che ornamento significa.

La grazzia di questo Mondo, e di questo ornamento, è la Bellezza, alla quale, subitamente, che
quell' Amore fù nato, tirò, e condusse la Mente
Angelica, la quale essendo brutta, per suo mezzo,
bella divenne.   I. ii

38   Finalmente in tutti, l'Amore accompagna il
Caos, e va innanzi al Mondo: desta le cose che
dormono: le tenebrose illumina: da vita alle cose
morte: forma le non formate: e dà perfezione alle'mperfette. Dalle quali lodi quasi nessuna mag-
giore si puo dire, o pensare.   I. ii

39   E questa spezie divina, cio è Bellezza, in tutte le
cose l'Amore, cio è desiderio di se, ha procreato.
Imperocchè fe Dio a se rapisce il Mondo, e'l
Mondo è rapito da lui, un certo continuo attrai-
mento è tra Dio, e'l Mondo: che da Dio comincia,
e nel Mondo trapassa, e finalmente in Dio termina:
e come per un certo cerchio d'onde si partì ritorna.
Si che un cerchio solo, e quel medesimo da Dio nel
Mondo: e dal Mondo in Dio: ei tre modi si
chiama. In quanto ei comincia in Dio, e alletta,
Bellezza: in quanto ei passa nel mondo, e quel
rapisce, Amore: In quanto mentre che ei ritorna
nell'Autore, a lui congiunge l'Opera sua, Dilettazione. L'Amore adunque, cominciando dalla Bellezza, termina in dilettazione. . . . E necessario è,
che l'Amore sia buono, conciosia che egli nato da
Bene si ritorni in Bene. Perche quel medesimo Dio
è la Bellezza, Il quale tutte le cose desiderano: e
nella cui possessione tutte si contentano, si che qui
il nostro desiderio s'accende. Qui l'ardore degli
Amanti si riposa: non perche, si spenga, ma perche
egli si adempie.   II. ii

41   Adunque un medesimo volto di Dio riluce i tre
specchi posti, per ordine, nell'Angelo, nell'Animo,

e nel corpo mondano: Nel primo come piu pro-
pinquo, in modo chiarissimo: nel secondo come piu
remoto, men chiaro: nel terzo, come remotissimo,
molto oscuro.

41 Perlaqualcosa tutte le parti del mondo: perche
sono opera d'uno artefice, e membri d'una medisima
macchina tra se in essere e vivere simile per una
scambievole Carità insieme si legano. In modo,
che meritamente si puo dire, l'Amore Nodo
perpetuo, legame del Mondo, e delle parti sue
immobil sostengo, e dell'universa Macchina fermo
fondamento.   III. iii

44 . . . e si rivolgono in un celeste e lucido velame:
nel quale rivolti, nelli corpi terreni si rinchiuggono.
Perche l'ordine naturale richiedi, che l'animo
purissimo, non si congiunga a questo corpo im-
purissimo, se non per mezzo d'un puro velame, il
quale essendo men puro che l'animo, è stimato da
Platonici comodissima copula dell' Animo, col
corpo terreno.   VI. iv

44 La forza di questi doni, Dio principalmente in se
contiene: Dipoi concede questa alli sette Dii, che
muovono li setti Pianeti, e da noi si chiamono
Angeli sette, che intorno al trono di Dio si rivolgono: In modo che ciascuni ricevono d'un dono,
piu che d'un'altro secondo la proprietà di loro
natura. . . .   VI. iv

Qualunque animo, sotto lo'mpero di Giove nel
corpo terreno descende, concepe nel discendere una
certa figura di fabbricare uno huomo conveniente
alla stella di Giove: la qual figura, nel suo corpo
celeste, che è ottimamente adatto a riciverla, molto
propria scolpisce. E se similmente arà trovato la
terra temperato seme, ancora in quello dipinge
terza figura, molto simile alla seconda, e alla prima.
E s'e' truova il contrario non sara simile. Spesso

avviene, che due animi sarano discesi, regnante
Giove, benche in vari tempi: e l'uno di loro essendo
abbatuto in terra a seme adatto perfettamente arà
figurato il corpo suo, secondo quelle Idee di prima.
Ma l'altro avendo trovato Matteria inetta, arà
pure incomminciata la medisima opera, ma non
l'arà adempiuta con tanta similitudine ad esemplo
di se medesimo.   VI. vi

Onde nasce, che ciascuno massimamente ama,
non qualunque è bellissimo, ma ama i suoi: dico
quegli che hanno avuta natività cosimile: ancora
ch'e' non fussero cosi belli, come molti altri. E
pero si come abbiamo detto, coloro che sono nati
sotto una medesima Stella, sono in tal modo
disposti, che la immagine del piu bello di loro,
entrando per gli occhi nell' animo di quell'altro,
interamente si confà, con una certa immagine,
formata dal principio di essa generazione, cosi nel
velame celeste dell'Anima, come nel seno dell'anima.
. . . Di qui nasce, che egli Amanti sono stato
ingannati, ch'e giudicano la persona amata esser
piu bella, ch'ella non è. Imperocche in processo di
tempo e'no veggon la cosa amata nella propria immagine presa per li sensi: ma veggono quella immagine già formata dalla loro anima, a similitudine
della loro Idea.   VI. vi

47   La prima Venere, che abbiamo nominata, che è
nella Mente Angelica si dice esser nata di Celio
senza Madre: Perche la Materia da' Fisici è
chiamata Madre: E quella Mente è aliena dalla
corporale Materia. La seconda Venere, che nel-
l'Anima del Mondo si pone, di Giove e di Dione,
è generata: Di Giove cioè di quella virtù dell'Anima
mondana: la quale virtù muove i Ciele. Imperocchè
tal virtù ha creato quella potenzia, che le cose
inferiori genera. Dicono ancora questa Venere aver

Madre, per cagione che essendo ella infusa nella Materia del Mondo, pare che con la Materia s'accompagni. Finalmente per arrecare in somma, Venere, è di due ragioni: una è quella intelligenzia, laquale nella Mente Angelica ponemmo: l'altra è la forza del generare, all'Anima del Mondo attribuita. L'una e l'altra, ha l'Amore simile, e se compagno. Perche la prima per Amore naturale a considerare la Bellezza di Dio è rapita: La seconda è rapita ancora per il suo Amore, a creare la divina Bellezza ne'corpi Mondani. La prima abbraccia prima in se lo splendore divino: dipoi diffonde questo alla seconda Venere. Questa Seconda trasfonde nella Materia del Mondo le scintille dallo splendore gia ricevuto. . . . II. vii

48   Quando la Bellezza del corpo umano si rappresenta agli occhi nostri, la nostra Mente laquale è in noi la prima Venere ha in reverenzia, e in amore la detta Bellezza, come immagine dell'ornamento divino: e per questa a quello 'spesse volte si desta. Oltre a questo la potenzia del generare, che è Venere in noi seconda, appetisce di generare una forma a questa simile. Adunque in amendue queste potenzie è l'Amore: Il quale nella prima, è desiderio di contemplare: nella seconda è desiderio di generare bellezza. L'uno e l'altro Amore è onesto, seguitano l'uno e l'altro divina immagine. Or che è quello che Pausania nell'Amore vitupera? Io velo dirò. Se alcuno, per grande avidità di generare pospone il contemplare, o veramente attende alla generazione per modi indebiti, o veramente antepone la Pulcritudine del corpo a quella dell'Anima: costui non usa bene la degnità d'Amore.   II. vii

49   . . . e però la Mente dalla'nquisizione della propria luce, a recuperar la luce divina è mossa, e allettata: e tale allettamento è il vero Amore.   IV. v

49 Diqui si conchiude, che l'amore a cosa incorporale si riferisce: ed essa Bellezza è piutosto una certa spiritual similitudine delle cose, che spezie corporale. V. iii

49 S'e'ci piaceranno i Corpi, gli Animi, gli Angeli, non ameremo questi proprii, ma Dio in questi. Ne' corpi ameremo l'ombra di Dio: ne gli Animi la similitudine di Dio: ne gli Angeli la immagine di Dio. Così nel tempo presente ameremo Dio in tutte le cose: acciocche finalmente amiamo tutte le cose in lui. VI. xix

139 Amore è libero, e spontaneamente nasce nella libera volontà, la quale ancora Dio non constringerà: perche da principio ordinò la volontà dovere esser libera. Si che Amor fa forza a ognuno: e non riceve da alcuno violenza. V. viii

154 La Bellezza è un certo atto, ovvero raggio di quindi per tutto penetrante: Prima nell' Angelica Mente: poi nell' anima dell' Universo, e nell' altre Anime: Terzo nella Natura: Quarto nella Materia de' corpi ... Cosi qualunque considera l'ornamento in questi quattro, Mente, Anima, Natura, e Corpo: ed esso ama: certamente il fulgore di Dio in questi, e per detto fulgore esso Dio vede, e ama. II. v

APPENDIX III

Pico della Mirandola's Version of the Ascent

Pico della Mirandola does not include the seventh stage of the ascent, that of divine union. This was, however, its recognized culmination—"the Sabbath of the soul" following six days of labour—and it is possible that he omitted it because, having had one collision with the Holy Office, he was being particularly careful to avoid another. This version occurs in his Commentary on Benivieni's *Canzona dello Amore Celeste et Divino*, 1487, and is, in spite of his quarrel with Ficino, mainly of Marsilian derivation. I give below the seventeenth-century translation by Thomas Stanley, entitled *A Platonick Discourse upon Love*, 1651, which is available, edited by E. G. Gardner, in The Humanist's Library, vol. VII, 1914.

From Material Beauty we ascend to the first Fountain by six Degrees:

1. The Soul through the sight represents to her self the Beauty of some particular Person, inclines to it, is pleased with it, and while she rests here, is in the first, and most imperfect material degree.

2. She reforms by her imagination the Image she hath received, making it more perfect as more spiritual; and separating it from Matter, brings it a little nearer Ideal Beauty.

3. By the light of the agent Intellect abstracting this Form from all singularity, she considers the Universal Nature of Corporeal Beauty by it self: this is the highest degree the Soul can reach whilst she goes no further than Sense.

4. Reflecting upon her own Operation, the knowledge of universal Beauty, and considering that every thing founded in Matter is particular, she concludes this universality proceeds not from the outward Object, but her Intrinsecal Power: and reasons thus: If in the dimme Glasse of Material Phantasmes this Beauty is represented by vertue of my Light, it follows that, beholding it in the clear Mirrour of my substance devested of those Clouds, it will appear more perspicuous: thus turning into her self, she finds the Image of Ideal Beauty communicated to her by the Intellect, the Object of Celestiall Love.

5. She ascends from this Idea in her self, to the place where Celestial Venus is, in her proper form: Who in fullness of her Beauty not being comprehensible, by any particular Intellect, she, as much as in her lies, endeavours to be united to the first Minde, the chiefest of Creatures, and general Habitation of Ideal Beauty.

6. Obtaining this, she terminates, and fixeth her journey; this is the sixth and last degree.

One Light flowing from God, beautifies the Angelick, the Rational Nature, and the Sensible World.

INDEX

INDEX

223

INDEX

Printed in Great Britain
by T. and A. CONSTABLE LTD., Hopetoun Street
Printers to the University of Edinburgh

1906